Discipline and Integration in the Catholic College

(The proceedings of the Workshop on Discipline and Integration in the Catholic College, conducted at the Catholic University of America from June 9th to June 20th, 1950)

Edited by

ROY J. DEFERRARI, PH.D., LL.D., L.H.D., ED.D.

THE CATHOLIC UNIVERSITY OF AMERICA PRESS
Washington 17, D. C.
1951

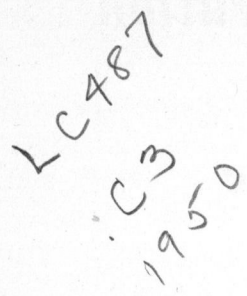

COPYRIGHT 1951
THE CATHOLIC UNIVERSITY OF AMERICA PRESS, INC.
PRINTED IN U.S.A.

Manufactured by
Universal Lithographers, Inc.
Baltimore, Md.
U. S. A.

Foreword

The Catholic University of America is happy to present herewith the proceedings of its fifth annual workshop on the various phases of Catholic higher education. In the "Foreword" of the proceedings of the Workshop on Catholic higher education held in 1949, we had occasion to say: "The Workshop, of which the proceedings are presented herewith, has succeeded chiefly, we believe, in clarifying the nature and scope of integration as we have just defined it, and possibly in offering reasonable solutions of the more important practical preliminary difficulties. The details for the execution of this integration in individual fields have only been touched upon. More study, in part at least, through more specialized workshops needs to be carried on."

Thus the Workshop of 1950 dealt with a special aspect of the general subject of Integration in Catholic Colleges and Universities, namely, Discipline and Integration in the Catholic College. Of course, by discipline we mean here every disciplinary phase of life in college that affects the body, the mind, and the soul, i.e., the whole man.

The arrangement of this volume follows, on the whole, that of its predecessors. The Table of Contents contains a list of the subjects of the discussions and the seminars, also a detailed description of the nature of the subjects of the discussions. The first part presents the main treatment of each subject and the second part, the summaries of the specialized studies conducted in the seminars. The third and final part consists of a special feature of the workshop, a much needed paper on archives, and of a list of the members of the Workshop and the institutions represented by them.

Mr. John Julian Ryan has made his usual important contribution to the success of this workshop. We are most grateful to him. We are also grateful to Miss Rita Watrin, Assistant to the Secretary General, who continues to make herself more and more indispensable to the Secretary General's office.

ROY J. DEFERRARI, *Director of Workshops*

Table of Contents

Page

FOREWORD III

PART I

General Conferences on Discipline and Integration in the Catholic College

A GENERAL EXPLORATION OF THE PROBLEM OF DISCIPLINE AND INTEGRATION 3
John Julian Ryan, A. B., Conception, Missouri

> The false view of education is that it is a gymnastic acquisition of a variey of "readinesses" for a necessarily chaotic world of catch-as-catch-can. Presumably, the student, motivated by self-reliance, by the spur of competition, and by the desire for self-aggrandizement, is to acquire, under fairly Epicurean surroundings and "laboratory conditions," the pragmatic, positivistic, or scholastic formulae necessary for "success." The intellectual discipline here consists largely of five-finger exercises and piece-meal memorizing, as the moral consists largely of avoiding penalties and submitting to drills.
>
> This talk will be an attempt to show what kind of discipline is implied by the proper Christian view of education as against the false view: what are the conditions required for assuring sound Catholic discipline in the best sense of the word; and how are we to change our present methods, if necessary, in order to assure these conditions?

DISCIPLINE, INTEGRATION, AND METHODS OF STUDY .. 16
Willis Dwight Nutting, B. Litt. (oxon), Ph.D., University of Notre Dame, Notre Dame, Indiana

> Since, in any sound apprenticeship, most of the work falls on the student, as most of the direction and inspiration fall on the teacher, it is right that the sudent should be given training in methods of study. This talk will therefore be concerned with the main principles of such training; that is, with methods of familiarization, of procedure from crude to refined perform-

ance, of cogitation, of conscious assimilation, of perfection by revision, of thoughful practice, etc. The talk will raise such questions as these: Should not the student be examined for his methods of work, as well as for his performances and his ability to reproduce the matter of what he has learned? Should he not have available to him various kinds of "work clinics"? Should not students be trained to work together, in classrooms and out of them (as well as individually)? Should the student not be marked for cooperative endeavor (through the giving of one mark to whole groups, as groups)? Should he not be given at least one course during every year at night, so as to accustom him to the use of the time most available for study in later life?

DISCIPLINE AND THE CASE METHOD 32
Reverend Paul Hanly Furfey, Ph.D., The Catholic University of America, Washington, D. C.

There is no better way of encouraging students than that of convincing them that the training they are receiving is immediately practical. For that reason, this talk will deal with such questions as: Cannot the student be taught to use all forms of activity, from that of the Sodality to that of the dramatic or the debating society, as opportunities for putting into practice the theories learned in the regular course? Should he not be tested for his ability to apply his knowledge wherever it does apply in solving the real and systematically more and more difficult cases that arise in his own home, parish, college, town, etc.; this, as a source of hope, as well as of practice? Should not every teacher, therefore, be expected to know enough about all these parochial, domestic, collegiate, civic, etc. forms of activity to use the cases they afford, as well as those given in textbooks, for analysis and solution?

DISCIPLINE, MARKS, REWARDS, AND PUNISHMENTS . . . 44
Willis Dwight Nutting, B. Litt. (oxon), Ph.D., University of Notre Dame, Notre Dame, Indiana

It is right that students should possess at all times a clear and just notion of their rate of progress. Also, they should enjoy the rewards of good work and suffer due punishments for poor. But any use of marks, honors, demerits, and the like depends properly on correct answers to questions like the following: Is it possible—or how possible is it—to measure quality of work by quantitative units? Should we mark all courses in a liberal arts college primarily as arts, and only secondarily as sciences: should we mark primarily for skill acquired, and only secondarily for knowledge reproducible? Should a student be marked early in a course for the very skill he has come to acquire; and should the marks that he then gets be averaged into his final grade? How can we make sure that a student who gets a C will be master of all the *essential* doctrines of a course and all the *essential* kinds of skill it develops, rather than master of some which are essential and some which are not? Should we prefer the mode to the average? How can we discourage the mere getting of marks and yet make sure that our students "make a good showing"? Should not rewards be in the form of opportunity for more instruction or of books in the field in which proficiency was shown? Should the student be rewarded by freeing him from routine and compulsory attendance—by treating him as responsible and mature? Should not punishment consist of deprivation of privileges of attending class, using the library, etc., along with deprivation of pastimes and of participation in activities? Is competition an acceptable motive in Christian education?

DISCIPLINE AND THE REALIZATION OF ITS NECESSITY .. 56
Sister M. Honora, Ph.D., Marygrove College, Detroit, Michigan

No one willingly embraces a course of hard training unless he feels challenged by the need to do what that training is for and unless the training itself seems necessitated rather than imposed arbitrarily. The student must therefore be shown the *realistic, clear,* and *unified* objectives set for him by the full range of the Encyclicals—so that he can respond to *definite* challenges. But he must also realize—that is, feel as well as see—why, under the circumstances, the curriculum, the pedagogy, the disciplinary methods of his college have come to be what they are of necessity. This talk will therefore raise such questions as the following: Should not the teachers of each subject keep the students always mindful of its ultimate, as well as its immediate, purposes (not its "justification")? Should not every student be made to see, that is, the pertinence of each course and of each disciplinary method both to his general fourfold vocational ends and to his own special vocation?—and the pertinence of each part of each course to the course as a whole? Should he not know the architectonics and the history of his instruction and discipline? Can we do all these things by giving him some direct appreciation of what it is to run a school: as by giving him real teaching assignments and real disciplinary assignments at least as heavy as those given to the youngsters of Boys' Town?

DISCIPLINE AND LEADERSHIP PRESTIGE 69

Reverend Paul Hanly Furfey, Ph.D., The Catholic University of America, Washington, D. C.

> Since no one would ever train himself for a task he felt required heroism under those in whom he did not repose great trust, the student must be reminded, by everything his teachers do, that they are competent trustworthy masters of three things: 1) the arts they are asking him to master; 2) the sciences these arts imply; and 3) the art of teaching him both.
>
> This talk will deal therefore with the following considerations: What changes does a regard for these threefold abilities suggest in teaching training and selection? Does not a proper estimate of the complexity of their task mean that teachers themselves should welcome searching criticism by supervisors? Must they not manifest at all times a sense of the sacredness of wisdom and of their function as teachers? Must they not, for that reason as well as for other reasons, maintain an unvarying attitude of professional courtesy? Must they not treat their students with the courtesy suggested by their all being fellow-members of Christ—must they not show the student that they think of him primarily as someone to "be brought to himself" as a Christian, an *alter Christus* of whom one has therefore a right always to expect great things? Does all this imply a course in Christian courtesy in the training of teachers and students alike?

DISCIPLINE, INTEGRATION, AND WORRY 80

Marie A. Corrigan, M.A., The Catholic University of America, Washington, D. C.

> Since it is obvious that a student who is worried about being clumsy, unpopular, poorly dressed, lower class, incapable of making expenses meet, troubled by religious doubt, infatuated, etc., cannot be a good student, we must consider what the best methods are for at least lessening these personal, social, economic, educational, and religious worries. How free of such worries must the student feel in order to get most of the benefits, if not all the benefits, of a liberal educa-

vii

tion? How can students be guided into aiding one another in these matters? Should not Catholic Action begin at college itself? Can class distinctions be levelled by uniforms or other devices? How can the student be made to feel "cared for" by all kinds of people at all times?

DISCIPLINE, INTEGRATION, AND THE CONDITIONS OF LEISURE 95

John Julian Ryan, A.B., Conception, Missouri

If it is true that the student will not learn properly unless he has the time and the peace necessary for investigation, for Socratic discovery, for practice, for familiarization and maturization, for aesthetic appreciation, for meditation and for contemplation of his various subjects, it would seem vital for us to consider the following questions: Can we reduce the number of studies in college or the length of time to be spent on some of them? Should we teach only the essentials of each subject, though, of course, thoroughly? How can we assure habits of hard, but unworried, work, as well as give time for extra-classroom activities? Should we not, as a measure for sound moral integration, stress heavily the requirement that basic things should be well done—handwriting, note-taking, speaking, reading, the giving of clear, exact answers, the writing of unexceptionable reports—and never accept slovenly brilliance in their stead? How, in short, can we preserve the values both of thoroughness and of leisure?

DISCIPLINE AND UNITY OF ATMOSPHERE 110

Dom Hilary Martin, O.S.B., B.S. in Arch., Master in City Planning, Portsmouth Priory, Portsmouth, Rhode Island

There are many ways by which we may demoralize our students. We may be illogical and inconsistent in policy and practice, as when, for instance, we speak of the importance of religion while in fact denying its importance by emphasizing secular courses more than religious. Or we may set tasks that cannot produce the ends desired and then indulge in "charitable forgiveness" of "failure." We may lay down harsh restrictions and then deal weakly with those who break them.

But it is no less demoralizing for us to surround students with an atmosphere that does not foster the leisure, peace, asceticism, and spiritual joy suited to the Christian training they are being given. If it is demoralizing to tell students that, according to the *Mediator Dei,* the sung Mass is the ideal one and then not train him to sing or, worse still, let him develop slovenly habits of singing and lose interest in it, so is it also demoralizing to call upon students to adopt a heroic attitude and then surround them with effeminate representations of Our Lord or, for that matter, of her who was called "terrible as an army in array." Must we therefore not make sure that at least we do not devitalize our teaching by our carelessly sanctioned architecture (especially, perhaps, our classrooms, our dining rooms, our dormitories, and our gymnasiums), our sculpture, our paintings, even our textbooks and blackboards. What principles are we to follow if we are not to suggest to students that they are something other than what they are—or that they are doing something other, and less heroic and joyful, than what they are doing?

DISCIPLINE AND ASCETICISM 121

Reverend Edmond Darvil Benard, S.T.D., Ph.D., The Catholic University of America, Washington, D. C.

The first need of every soldier in the Church Militant is twofold. He must have a sufficiently lofty understanding of the function of Catholic education and of his position as a student to be inspired thereby. And he must be well enough habituated to the modes of grace-filled thinking, willing, and acting to be, in the full sense, a *trained* Christian.

This talk will therefore deal with such questions as the following: What is a sound ascetical life and what relation to such living does Catholic education bear? Since the Christian virtues are supernatural habits, how are they reinforced and implemented by the "natural" acquired habits, and what is the role of Catholic educational discipline in the acquisition of the latter? What about training in the sound asceticism of the Liturgy and of the devotions subsidiary to it? What about the dangers of "compulsion"?

Regarding matters of practice: Should there not be a month long orientation course (and no other) at the beginning of each year? Can retreats be used as miniature substitutes for such a course? Cannot the initiation into college be "solemnized" through a retreat-like training which would purge the student of false theories of education and acquaint him with its true significance? Should there not be regular faculty meetings for the purpose of enabling instructors to gain an ever fuller understanding of the interlocking relationship involved in this question of discipline and asceticism?

PART II

Summaries of Seminar Proceedings

ON TEACHING ENGLISH COMPOSITION INTEGRATEDLY 137
    Directed by John Julian Ryan, A.B., Conception, Missouri

ON INTEGRATING THE SOCIAL SCIENCES 152
    Directed by Reverend Paul Hanly Furfey, Ph.D., The Catholic University of America, Washington, D. C.

ON INTEGRATING EPISTEMOLOGY, COSMOLOGY, CHEMISTRY, AND PHYSICS 156
    Directed by Reverend Leo A. Foley, S.M., Ph. D., The Catholic University of America, Washington, D. C.

ON INTEGRATING BIOLOGY, PSYCHOLOGY, NATURAL THEOLOGY, LITURGY 164
    Directed by Kenneth E. Anderson, Ph.D., St. Bonaventure College, St. Bonaventure, New York, and Reverend Henry E. Wachowski, M.S., The Catholic University of America, Washington, D. C.

ON INTEGRATING LANGUAGES AND LITERATURES 169
    Directed by Helmut A. Hatzfeld, Ph.D., The Catholic University of America, Washington, D. C.

PART III

Appendixes

Appendix A: THE ARCHIVES OF A CATHOLIC COLLEGE OR UNIVERSITY 179
    Reverend Henry J. Browne, Ph.D., The Catholic University of America, Washington, D. C.

Appendix B: MEMBERS OF THE WORKSHOP AND INSTITUTIONS REPRESENTED 195

PART I

The General Conferences on Discipline and Integration in the Catholic College

A General Exploration of the Problem of Discipline and Integration

By John Julian Ryan

The problem of discipline will be dealt with in this paper as related to the problem of integration. Accordingly, I will not concern myself here with a discussion of such particular matters as the cutting of classes, the use of a demerit system, policies of suspension and expulsion, the qualifications of a dean of discipline, and the like; rather, I will try simply to explore—and, even so, not explore fully—what might be called the basic or philosophic problems to be met with in any correlative study of integration and discipline.

I will therefore begin by reviewing very briefly what I proposed in the Workshop of last year as an ideal of integrative training; then I will try to make out what measures of discipline (intellectual as well as voluntary) such a training implies; and finally, I will suggest what kinds of changes in attitude and technique may be required of us by the adoption of these measures.

In the Workshop of last year, I proposed as the ideal principle of integration that of Christian practicality—this, of course, being understood in its deepest and most liberal sense. This principle was there shown to imply a method essentially militant, in the same sense in which the Church may be described as the Church Militant. And its end was that already set up in previous workshops—that of making every student, regardless of future occupation or status, into the particular kind of priest-prophet-maker-ruler he was called to be.

The training proposed would be militant in that the teachers "would consider their task to be that of enabling every student to work out, in every field, an intelligent estimate of the situation in which mankind finds itself at all times and at the present day; they would show him how to gain a clear understanding of the obstacles to be met, of the enemies inner and outer to be overcome, of favorable forces and conditions, of possible methods of attack, and of plans for sound campaigns. They would aid the student thus to outline the problems to be overcome, to select the most important, and to determine which of these he should be able to solve by the end of each course and of the whole four years of training. Then they would arrange practice periods for the acquirement of this or that skill and this or that combination of skills, as these are called for in the solving of the problems (which would be made, throughout the four years, increasingly harder, larger, and subtler).

Naturally, these problems were to be limited in number and kind for several reasons: first, it takes time to develop any habit of skillful action; second, although all problems should be real, concrete, and particular, they are a waste of time if they are merely peculiar and ephemeral. They must be concrete but *typical;* not just this problem and then that, but an *instance* of this kind of problem which naturally leads into and aids in the solution of an *instance* of that kind of problem. They should, in other words, form a "case system" similar to, but superior to, that used today in many law schools.

Thus, to give an example or so, the student taking up the course in participation in the Mass might well be asked, first off, what he thought was the ideal way of "going to Mass" and be required to give a full impromptu answer to this question. Next, he might be required to read the *Mediator Dei* and asked to revise his theory in the light of this Encyclical. Thereupon, he could be required, with some guidance, to work out an "estimate of the situation" for himself, his fellow-students, his own parish and the Church: to determine what the spread between the actual and the ideal is. Then he should be encouraged to work out what ought to be done (prudently and charitably of course) to lessen that spread; specifically, what he himself must do to master the art of corporate worship and to help others to do so.

Or again, when the student takes up economics, he should be put through a similar training: being asked to tell what he thinks is wrong with our economic situation, to check his opinion by the *Rerum Novarum* and the *Quadragesimo Anno,* to make up plans for remedying the situation in accordance with the objectives and guiding principles of these works, to check these plans by those set forth by the Distributists, the Cooperativists and the proponents of "Industry Council Method" (the Bishops of the United States), as well as those set forth by anti-Christian or agnostic economists. (Naturally, the working out of problems such as those given in these two examples would run concurrently with the whole course in question.)

Ideally, the teachers as practicing artists in each field would be able to give the kinds of guidance, set the kinds of problems, and raise the kind of theoretitical issues which, because they are crucial, would evoke the keenest interest. They could, in fact, set real problems which the students knew and felt to be real—any answers to which, even the guesses of students, would be at least indirectly or negatively helpful, with the result that students could realize that they were, even in their mere practice periods or most tentative essays, making some contribution to the furthering of Christendom. They could feel from the outset that they were not undergoing a mere series of drills, but a true, realistic, valuable apprenticeship, differing from that of carpenter or plumber, lawyer or doctor, only in being concerned with more basic problems than are these fellow craftsmen.[1]

What, then, are the disciplinary requirements of such a system of training? We answer this question properly, I believe, when we answer the following series of questions into which it can be broken down:

1. What must we do to meet the disciplinary requirements of training the student to perform any one act of skill?
2. What is further required to make the skillful performing of it habitual—to give the student the virtue for it?
3. What are the similar requirements—and what must we do to meet them—of any *course* of training which will enable the student to gain more and more skill in dealing with the major problem of some one given liberal art?
4. What are the requirements of any *system* of such courses of training?
5. What *specific* forms do these various requirements take in the training of the student in each of his functions: as priest; as prophet; as maker; and as ruler?
6. What relations of proportion and order should exist between these various functions and the kinds of disciplinary training they require?

---

[1] Roy J. Deferrari, ed, *Integration in Catholic Colleges and Universities* (Washington, D. C.: Catholic University of America Press, 1950), pp. 18-19.

7. Finally, what general changes should we therefore consider in teaching methods; choice of teachers; teacher training; methods of grading and certification; scheduling; handling of extra-classroom activities; customs and regulations; equipment and atmosphere?

First, then, what are the typical disciplinary requirements to be met in the training of a student to perform any one act skillfully, even once? They can be listed, I think, as follows:

We are concerned with aiding him
1. to acquire enthusiasm, awaking his desire to perform the act and the hope that he can do so;
2. to orient himself and focus on the inevitable determinants of the act;
3. to investigate and attain a sharp image of the act, in its stages and as a whole;
4. to perfect—to finish well or to formulate unexceptionably; and
6. to appreciate his act, the product of it and the science of it, and to correlate it with others as well as to integrate it into a large system of practice and theory.

Now, if we consider each of these again in turn, we may be able to make out, through a concrete example, what each of these requirements implies specifically. Let us suppose, then, for the sake merely of a fair case, that a teacher of economics were to set out to train a student to perform properly some one act in a liberal art—let us say, the act of solving the problem raised by the Christian doctrine of poverty. Suppose a teacher wishes the student to go through the process, if only once, of giving a sound answer to the question: What must I myself do to eliminate or to try to eliminate from my own life and from the lives of my fellow Americans the corrupting force of luxury and to help substitute for it a sound Christian poverty? With such a problem before us, we are easily enabled to see the necessity for and the nature of the disciplinary requirements previously listed.

Enthusiasm. Obviously if the student is to make the effort to solve this problem well, he must be roused to do so enthusiastically; and this, both negatively and positively.

Negatively, he must be made to feel horror at the heinousness of the crimes committed in the name of luxury, tragic fear and pity for those who commit them, disgust and indignation at waste, fear of the Lord at the realization of the retribution which may have to be suffered from this literally sinful waste (in which the student himself may well have been a participant). Positively, the student should be made to feel compassion for those who live in destitution, gratitude toward Our Lord and to saint upon saint who have called upon mankind to shun luxury, joy at the beauty of Lady Poverty and at the beauty of the lives of those who have followed her—all this, of course, without any hatred of those who love luxury, or any youthful impatience, bitterness, or holier-than-thou complacency.

Naturally, this means that, ideally at least, the beauty of Christian poverty should be caused to radiate to the students through everything with which they come in contact: the teacher's appearance, the kinds of advice he gives when asked about future work, his own obvious abhorrence of luxury and appreciation of poverty, etc. So, too, must the lesson be brought home by everything from the beautifully simple curriculum (beautiful because Christianly simple) which is designed for a life of Christian poverty, to customs, buildings, equipment, textbooks.

Orientation. In the next requirement, we meet especially the need for disciplining the student as a *person*, that is, as someone determinable. Here he is "facing off" to his problem as he would "face off" to a fence he had to climb. And he must be permitted to focus, gage, identify, estimate, reach his own tentative conclusion, with no sense of arbitrary compulsion. He should be encouraged to think out for himself and talk out with others, who are as new to the problem as he himself, its factors, determinants, *loci*, co-variants, being guided socratically, without consultation of books or teachers, through the collecting of examples, the devising of hypothetical crucial instances, the classification of these, the distinguishing of concepts, the inventing of terminology, the defining and evaluating and the assimilating of principles. He must here be guided (disciplined) to risk making a fool of himself (in humility); to cooperate charitably with others; to be patient with them as well as with himself at the inevitable fumbling, the snap judgments, the crude over-simplifications into which all beginners fall.

In this way, to return to the case in point, the student would come to realize, for example, at least the necessity for distinguishing between destitution and poverty; between a vocation and a mere money-making occupation; between indifference and true detachment; between property used in a stewardship and property abused in a so-called absolute ownership. He would estimate roughly the effect of luxury loving on our production, exchange, and distribution of goods, as well as on our political, social, and religious life. Finally, he would make out, at least dimly, what he himself is called upon to do in the light of these estimates. He would experience what it is to explore and map out a problem and to recognize its inevitable minimum implications.

The one great value, from the point of view of discipline, that is assured by this process of orientation is that of causing a student to see for himself the necessity of doing things which he would otherwise simply be commanded to do. He is made to face the acquisition of certain kinds of knowledge and skill as an objective requirement, not as in any sense an arbitrary one. He is taught to accept the exigencies of mere fact; and he begins to see the authorities over him as what their names signify, the "increasers" of his ability to deal with such fact.

Then, too, this arranging so that the facts dawn on him and so that he comes to grips with them easily and gradually, prevents his rushing into the makeshift techniques or short-cut methods that attain only immediate success. He is not hurried or startled into illiberalism—into the false practicality of the surprised mind.

Investigation. In this process, the student is to be trained in intellectual prudence primarily. He is to learn how to experiment, reason out, test, formulate the conclusion he has thus far arrived at, and then, and only then, to compare them with the answers of others. Here he is to be given the chance to train himself in fairness and accuracy as well as in thoroughness, learning what it is to take into account all possibilities, especially those that are distasteful. Morally, he is to be encouraged to be humble in acknowledging the inadequacy of his own concepts and plans; to be patient in accepting the nearest thing to a solution, and in never expecting to be fully rid of the pain of doubt; to be afraid of over-simplification or rationalization; to admire others and to adopt their ideas generously; to be ready in charity to appreciate the truth wherever it is to be found. He is to be given courage for taking the time to familiarize himself with the facts rather than simply to memorize them, and he is given the sense of leisure which makes investigation an apparent end in itself.

In the question dealt with here, then, he would thus learn what the classic utterances on and discussions of the problem of poverty have been—such as we find in Walter Shewring's *Rich and Poor in Christian Tradition*, and in more formal treatises in moral theology and ascetic theology as well as in books of sociology.

Invention. Here the student must be particularly trained in certain moral and intellectual virtues not always easy to put under their conventional categories.

He must have the courage to face the problem afresh, without turning to others for immediate aid, or proudly striving for a self-conscious and silly originality. Here, too, he must be humble enough to be willing to make a fool of himself. He must be zealous enough to persevere in doing a task himself and in working over it until it is well done, no matter how many revisions it requires. He must be patient with himself in failure, while holding himself strictly to his best. He must be anxious for perfection, but no proud perfectionist. He must be willing to wait out an idea. He must be cautious in trying to foresee difficulties and objections. He must be religious in the sense of taking responsibility for the defects of what he does, while seeing that the good in it is attributable to God. He must look not to rewards, but to the sanction of God and the satisfaction of others as well as to the joy to be taken in the beauty of things well done and in sound technique.

Here, of course, whatever method a student hits upon that will make it easy for him to live in poverty and help others to do so—whatever final plan he works out "on his own" must easily and obviously entail exercises of will in such a way as to promote the moral and spiritual qualities mentioned. But, like every other plan, it would also call for certain intellectual qualities as well. The student would need to set about his inventing in a craftsmanly way, that is with a certain orderliness, circumspection, flexible imaginativeness, tactful discursiveness, and intuitiveness. He would use all the powers required for visualizing, estimating, devising, contriving, sketching out, foreseeing, and revising. He would learn to think, as St. Thomas would say, *collatively*, and as Newman would say, *illatively*: bringing to bear what was pertinent for both insight and plan. Whatever else he learned, he would certainly learn, as no mere memorizer ever does, what is meant by true imitation rather than slavish and by freshness of attack rather than by originality.

Perfecting or formulating. Here the virtues would be mainly those which we normally associate with study. For here the student is primarily concerned with analyzing and memorizing the solutions of others and their lines of reasoning. He would be learning to obey rules of memorizing, those concerned with regularity, whole-before-part learning, over-learning, spaced recall, periodic resting, the making of associational links, etc., to say nothing of neatness, punctuality, accuracy and correctness. The moral qualities he would thus call into play are obviously those of justice and fortitude, here understood mainly as the willingness to meet obligations, to be fair, to give everything its due, to endure drudgery, and the like. Obviously, there is here also implied the necessity for the student to test theories for degrees of certitude and to become methodically skeptical without becoming a skeptic. Concretely, all this would mean that he would become a scholar of the subject of poverty.

Integration. Here the main intellectual virtues are obviously those of understanding and wisdom, the student being encouraged to discover the relations of poverty not only to all economic processes but also to all other processes of civilization—to the *mores* and the ascetic life of a people. What does poverty mean, not only to the production, the exchange, and the distribution of wealth, but to the customs, the codes, and the spiritual life of the nation? What happens if he himself and a million others like him get out of the habit of buying that extra chocolate bar? In answering such questions, the student will be encouraged to see luxury in relation to the whole plan of things; to see what is meant by legitimate pleasures; to observe how Catholicity answers this question in a way different from that of the pleasure seeker, the epicure, the stoic, or the Puritan. He will come to realize how any doctrine of this kind inevitably involves a host of others and always ends with questions of theology. The process of integration will also serve to train him in the virtues of religion and charity, causing him to connect all his actions with the "wholes" of which he is a part, with the Mystical Body, with the world, with the nation, with the parish, with the neighborhood. He should thus be made to feel his meaningfulness as a Christian person, and to realize his solidarity and co-responsibility with others. Finally, he can be made to feel the heroism of even the most obscure and "unimportant" a life.

If these are some, and I do not pretend that they are all, of the disciplinary requirements and the values of the training of a student in the performing of one assignment in a liberal art, the next consideration is: what would need to be done to make *habitual* the intellectual and moral dispositions involved herein.

Clearly, practice; but practice in the proper sense; not merely more and more knowledge of general principles, not merely practice in studying more and more facts or principles or interpretations, examples of other men's achievements or criticisms or analyses of implications. A growing knowledge of all these things would, to be sure, be highly desirable. But the practice I mean would consist, as I have said in the section quoted from the Workshop of last year, in the solving of many problems, problems increasingly "larger, more complex and subtler," demanding the use of more and more skill under conditions requiring greater and greater poise and address, with less and less guidance by the instructor. The student would be continuously challenged, but never strained, and his self-control would grow equally with his knowledge and understanding. He would be trained for performance, not for encyclopedic reproduction.

The other main disciplinary requirement for sound habits of practice is that of training the student to adjust himself properly to his difficulties, failures, and successes. He should be shown that there are, as Dom T. V. Moore has pointed out in his *Dynamic Psychology*, good forms of flight, compensation, defense, and sublimation and there are bad: and then he should be shown how he should avoid the bad and indulge properly in the good. Here he is to learn, in short, how to "take" himself and the results of his effort, much as athletes are taught how to take their achievements or their defeats. If, now, we look to the general requirements of any *course* or training, or any system of courses, we shall find, I think, that these requirements are pretty much the same as those of a single act and of the habit of performing it, which have been discussed thus far.

The difficulty here lies, as is to be expected, in the fact that a course has to be taught both as an art (a system of skills) and as a science (a system of knowledge). The training is thus to be governed both by the normal requirements of *growth in skill*, with due allowances for its spasmodic tempo, each student having his own rhythm of maturation, and by the requirements of *growth in knowledge*, which in turn often depend on the enthusiasm generated by growth in skill. But I believe that just as we can say that there are certain stages in learning to do a simple thing, we can also say that there are much the same stages in learning to perform a complex one or in mastering a combination of performances. And these stages can be reduced, for practical purposes, to four: that of motivation, that of familiarization, that of practice, and that of recapitulation (which last includes: explicit study, formulation, and integration). If this contention be granted, it follows that all our units of training must be arranged and disciplined accordingly. In each, the first stage must have mainly the discipline of spiritual cadetship; the second must have mainly the discipline of intellectual discourse and controversy—that of the agora or the forum; the next must have that of apprenticeship; and the last that of scholarship and discipleship.

All of which means by implication that we shall be training the priest-prophet-maker-rulers we should be training only if we arrange to give each of their four-fold functions a training which has its due stages, its due period of motivation, of familiarization, etc. The four years' training would therefore best be determined, as far as possible, with some general regard for this pattern. Thus, from a disciplinary point of view, something like the following might be desirable: There should be first an orientation course at the beginning of the whole four years, in which the whole pattern of education should be presented so as to rouse an apostolic enthusiasm for it and understanding of it. (I should be willing to have this course the sole one for as long as the first two months if necessary.) Such a course would be matched by one for "tying together" the whole education at the end of the four years, this one also to last for two months, final examinations having been taken at mid-years. As being closely related to enthusiasm, the courses having mainly to do with the functions of priest and prophet, courses in Christian worship, in history, in the philosophy of craftsmanship, in logic, and in the communicative arts and crafts should come earlier, when possible, than the others.

The courses having to do with ruling should come next, as being both orientative and normative. Those having to do with making, including the natural sciences, might come next; and those concerned with the final re-synthesis, philosophy and theology, might well come in last. Naturally, there would be no sharp demarcations here. In every year, there would be some science, some philosophy, some theology, and so on, but the emphases might vary, I should think, as just suggested.

Now, such a division of the whole training into stages, of each course into similar stages, and of each section of each course into similar minor stages—this would, no doubt, demand a great deal of revision of our methods and conceptions of discipline. Indeed, what this method implies for the training of the student as lay-priest alone would seem appallingly disruptive to many administrators. But disruptive or not, the questions it raises still have to be answered, such questions as: If the *Mediator Dei* says that the Sung Mass is the ideal form for active participation, must we not have it daily, and call on our students to master Gregorian chant and ecclesiastical Latin? What has been beautifully said by Father Francis X. Charnotta (*Catholic Art Quarterly*, Pentecost issue) of the Catholic musician is true of the student:

> (He) . . . owes it to himself to live in his own life the life of the Liturgy as thoroughly as he is able, to follow

the rhythm of each day of the Church with its center in the Mass, to follow the rhythm of her *week* where Sunday sheds its light and grace over the six days in its wake, to follow the rhythm of her *year* as the Christian pattern of life— a continuous living in the mysteries of our redemption. Truly, the problem of our Catholic way of life is not whether we live in the Church, but whether the Church lives in us.

And if all this is so, should we not have at least the collects or the hymn from the appropriate Day Hour said before and after each class? Should we not encourage the habit of prayer by causing the student to feel that the prie-dieu is as normal a part of his room as his desk or his bed? The answers to these and similar questions cannot help causing us to examine searchingly our theories of everything from the making out of schedules to the decorating of dining halls.

So, too, would the answers to many similar questions which could also be raised here concerning the training of the student as prophet or as maker or as ruler. It is sufficient, however, for us to observe that, if what I have been maintaining is sound, we face issues that will keep us busy for much longer than two weeks. For it is clear that, at the very least, we must strive to work out reasoned answers to the following questions: Must the liberal arts discipline here proposed be sacrificed because it will not permit us to "cover the ground"? because it takes too much time? because it requires a leisure that can easily be abused? because it requires the teacher to be a leader, as well as a master artist, scientist, and scholar, demanding of him a certain skill in blending various disciplines? Or must it be rejected for some other and better set of reasons?

Certainly, whether you agree with what I have been saying or not, it will have, I trust, at least the effect of focussing your attention on the inadequacies of any system of discipline which is based on the following beliefs:

1. that since a college is primarily a place for the training of the intellectual virtues, it is only very secondarily a place for the training of the whole Christian;
2. that intellectual training consists in getting a student to "take up," topic by topic, a subject that has been

broken down into purely logical units and arranged in a purely logical synthesis;
3. that the punctuality of the student, his class attendance, his deportment, his ability to conform to a regular schedule with on-the-dot acquisition of related items of information, his ability to take notes, to use the library, to compile, digest, and reproduce data—all these are proof that he is well-disciplined;
4. that the student with a well-stocked mind and regular habits of study is a liberal artist;
5. that moral and spiritual virtues are well enough instilled by indoctrination, by inspiration from occasional lecturers, by devotional practices, by the encouragement of various Catholic Action societies, and by the requirement of attendance at chapel some three times a week; and
6. that since the world was made for man and man was made to save his soul, that student is well-disciplined who, on graduation, sets out to save his soul by simply using the world and enabling others to do so, with little regard for his Christian duty to sacramentalize it.

At all events, if we do consider the systems of discipline here suggested; if we do place them properly side by side and observe them carefully; if we do discuss, frankly and freely, the conflicts between them—then we shall all, I believe, find this Workshop, *Deo volente,* a profound and profitable experience.

Discipline, Integration, and Methods of Study

By WILLIS DWIGHT NUTTING

We college teachers in this country are faced with a situation which is perhaps unique in the history of education. Students come to us for what they think to be (and what we claim to be) higher education, without having had much previous discipline in study, even in the three R's. They come to us with the juvenile attitude of the school boy toward his master, and they dare us to teach them anything. They come to us without being able to read a book or to explain themselves in writing. They come to us backed by their parents' expectation that a college education will transform them from something very crude into something highly polished and efficient. And they come, to a large extent, because we have urged them to come and have held out to them great promises of advantage to be gained.

For us Catholic college teachers the situation becomes still more unique by the fact that our students are in the great majority the first generation to seek higher education, and many of them come from homes of a foreign culture where literacy, if it exists, is in a foreign tongue.

We start then with a student body of which we can presume almost nothing in advance except that they will be thoroughly un-uniform in their preparation, in their backgrounds, and in their hopes. We can presume no definite body of knowledge and none of the special skills that secondary education is supposed to supply. I hasten to add that all this does not mean that the boys and girls who come to us lack all mental training. Far from it! Their sports and their jalopies and their gangs, their movies, radios and magazines have given them an alertness and an experience which have matured one side of them to a considerable degree. But their interest in and understanding of intellectual pursuits have been encouraged neither by their training nor by their environment. They have lived all their lives in a young people's world, where practically their only sanctions have been the approval and disapproval of their associates. Neither the birch rod nor a serious association with adult people has been employed to give them, by force or attraction, an introduction to the world of adult thinking men.

Such is the character of the body of freshmen who present themselves to us every September. History gives us no precedent in the methods of handling them. We must solve the problem ourselves. The problem is made more difficult by the educational aims that we have set for ourselves and for them.

In the first place we would like to produce scholars, people who as a result of our training will go out to extend the frontiers of knowledge and thereby win for themselves and for us the respect of the world of specialized learning. Our desires in this direction are enhanced by the fact that fat funds from the government and various private foundations are available for aiding graduate study in recognized schools. Then there is also the duty encumbent upon us, and the privilege, of enlarging the field of truth in every direction we can.

College teachers in general are enthusiastic about turning out replicas of what they believe themselves to be: experts in specialized fields of study. This reproductive urge is quite natural and also in line with a part of their duty. But they are not so enthusiastic about another one of the aims that their institutions have set for them: the turning out of men and women of high moral character who will be able to take their place as leaders of Christian society. It is the fashion for scholars to speak with contempt of "character education" as something on a lower level than their specialties. But even so we are committed to it by a thousand obligations. We are committed to it by what our catalogues and prospectuses promise; we are committed to it by what commencement speakers tell the high school graduates and by what our Catholic press urges upon parents. We are held to it by the expectation on the part of thousands of parents that the Catholic college is going to make something of their boys and girls. And incidentally, if these parents did not have this expectation and a willingness to trust us to fulfill it, our colleges would have to close for lack of support.

But these are not the only reasons for this educational

aim. We are also forced to it by the needs of the times. We are living in an age when the traditions, the values, the convictions, and the loyalties which have held Christian society together are dissolving, and there is the supreme necessity that they be in some way restored. But they can only be restored by explicitly teaching them in such a way that they will be rationally accepted by people as true. People no longer simply assume, for instance, that man is a spiritual being and of great dignity. They no longer take for granted the idea of justice and that it is the duty of society to enforce it. They no longer understand the obligation of service that goes with any excellence. These they must be shown, and the college is the place where they can be shown. This task of the college is vastly the most important, no matter what scholars may think.

At this point there will probably be some rather disdainful murmuring about silk purses and sow's ears. It is quite true that you cannot make the former out of the latter, but it is also true that silk purses are not the only valuable products within our range of intention. Since it is likely that most of our students, and students in general, would come under the sow's ear category, we might at least consider the possibility that extremely serviceable and beautiful leather wallets would be made out of them, wallets which would in the long run be more valuable than silk purses.

The task of "making something" of the mediocre student is laid upon us by the type of student we get, by the facts of life with regard to our survival, and by the needs of the times. It only remains for us to come down from our high horse of intellectual snobbishness and accept the task joyfully, realizing that what we are able to do for these students will perhaps have more impact on the world than our work with the scholars.

We are committed, then, to the type of college which takes in people who hope to be, and can be, scholars, and people who have no such ambitions and no such abilities, people who are entirely un-uniform in the discipline that they have had and of whom many have had no discipline at all. We can presume that they have at least average intelligence, that they are capable of improvement, and, being

Catholics, that some Christian appeal can reach most of them.

This is what we have to start with. The integrating and disciplining of the minds of these people present a very complex problem, one whose solution has not yet been worked out with any great success. We are faced not only with a diversity of mentalities but also with a diversity of goals. And this calls for a great variety of methods.

We must remember that the student's mind is the chief agent in the learning process. The teacher cannot "put" anything into that mind. The mind must "grasp" it for itself. But the teacher can inspire that mind, can guide it, and can even use various forms of pressure to incite it into activity. This supremacy of the student's mind in the process of learning means that no method used by the teacher can have more than tentative significance. It is tried subject to revision if it does not work in any particular case. The failure of a method in a given instance is not necessarily a reflection on the student or on the teacher, but the insistence on a method when it obviously does not work is certainly an evidence of a defect in the latter.

This means that the prevailing ideal of uniformity, according to which great masses of students are handled in convoys whose progress is measured by a conformity to certain standardized methods of teaching and examination, is thoroughly pernicious and contrary to the nature of man. To set up a couch of Procrustes, to which young minds must be fitted, if necessary by amputation or stretching, is simply an indication of man's inhumanity to man. The path to education is strewn with wreckage of the minds of intelligent boys and girls who did not happen to "click" with the methods used by their teachers.

But, you ask, how can a person teaching a course attended by thirty students vary the teaching method so as to suit each one? My answer is that it is just this impossibility which makes it imperative that the student be given wide opportunity to learn outside of so-called courses, But more of this later.

All the various educational aims that are gathered together in the ideology of a Catholic college contain one thing in common: they all assume that the student will be developed in one way or another, that we will "make something out of him." If this development does not take place, it were better had the student not come to us at all. And yet all of us have known seniors who were less interested in things of the mind and the things of the spirit and things of the Faith than they were when they came to us as freshmen. Somewhere in those four years, and probably in the first year, something very beautiful in them died. What is responsible?

Perhaps the key lies in this educational axiom: if we wish to aid in the development of the mind of a person who is old enough to have experienced his freedom as a human being, *we must arouse interest and willingness to co-operate before we apply pressure.* That there is a place for pressure is obvious, but pressure applied to a student who is not yet awake to any enthusiasm for becoming something that he is not is likely to arouse in him simply a sullen spirit of opposition which makes him anxious only to get by and get out. The opposition thus started can only grow when further pressures are put upon him. He becomes adept at avoiding the various kinds of punishments that we contrive for him, but he shows no interest, and he hates the subjects that he has been forced to study. This is not what we want. It can be the case with the very intelligent student as well as with the very dull.

Therefore, prior to discipline and integration there must be an awakening, and this holds true for the students who are potential scholars and those who are not. The sooner the awakening takes place the better, and our treatment of our freshmen might well be framed with this as a chief aim. Whether the arousing of interest in self-development can be accomplished by a definite technique is a matter for discussion, but not here. It may be a gift which some teachers have and others never will be able to acquire. At any rate, our freshmen should be given ample opportunity to associate with those teachers and to enter into those situations most likely to have a salutary effect in this regard. To insist on uniformity of method for freshmen while allowing much latitude of method for upper classmen is to deny experimentation where it is needed most—when we are trying to find out how to appeal to a person who has just newly come to us.

Once the student has accepted the idea that college offers a wonderful chance for improvement which he must take advantage of, he can see the purpose of an intellectual discipline and consent to it, at least in general intention. Then the various methods for training the mind can be applied with effect. And they should be applied with rigor if needed. But the methods will be various, for the educational background and the mentalities of the students are various.

The students who do not know how to read and how to write must be taught these fundamental accomplishments of the educated man. Here is room, I think, for methodological toughness: practice and practice and more practice in writing, with repeated revision until clearness is attained; and reading difficult books, slogging through them with a determination not to leave a single sentence uncomprehended, to "fight it out on this line if it takes all summer." All this is hard going, but it is a journey that every man who hopes to be educated must travel some time in his career, if not in high school, then in college. Judging by the freshmen that we get, we must agree that most of it has to be done in college. But a student who wants to make something of himself can see that he has to learn how to read and write, and no teacher should disdain to help him in the learning. Methodological toughness in the rhetorical arts must be exercised in history and zoology as well as in English. Clearness in expressing one's self and accuracy in comprehending the expression of another mind must be demanded everywhere.

The fundamental skills of reading and writing must be learned by hard work, and must be learned by all students. There is probably more excuse for uniformity of method here than anywhere else. But while this uniform teaching is going on, the students can in their other subjects be initiated into the great variety of ways in which knowledge can be acquired. Human minds are so different that there are scarcely two that work in the same way in learning. It is most important, therefore, that the student should be allowed as soon as possible to find out in what way he works best. If this is true, it is wrong in principle to lay out a plan of teaching whereby we use one method of teaching— usually one that amounts to a regimentation—for all freshmen. There may be as much difference in every way between two freshmen as there is between a freshman and a senior, and this difference must be reckoned with. It is much more than a difference between good and bad students. It is deeply psychological. It is by no means always the bad students that "get off on the wrong foot" in their freshman year because the method of teaching applied to them is not, in their case, a success.

We teachers differ as much among ourselves as the students do. Each of us has his own technique in teaching, a method which seems to work best for him. Each of us, therefore, has a unique way of introducing the young mind to a part of the realm of knowledge, and it is our duty by serious thought and work to perfect that way. I do not think it is our duty, however, to try to conform to a standardized technique in the interest of uniformity. This will be as disastrous for us as for the students.

If you will recall your own college days, you will remember that certain teachers had a great influence for good upon you. You will remember that there were other students who were not impressed with these particular teachers but had favorites of their own. And perhaps your favorites differed widely from each other in their teaching methods. All this illustrates the fact that no one technique, and no one personality can be successful for all students. None of us can expect one hundred percent success. But each one of us can hope to be successful with some.

This wide variety among teachers in technique and personality is a thing that can make a college a success as an educational institution, for it can supply a large range of possibilities for the student, so that he is much more likely to find a way of teaching that corresponds to his way of learning and can thus use to the best advantage the intellectual equipment with which he has been endowed.

Let us consider some of these types of successful teaching. On the one hand, there is the hard-boiled martinet, who starts out by scaring the students to death and aims to keep them on their toes throughout the course. He fails two-thirds of the class in the mid-semester exams. He demands accuracy in recitations. He is a regular top sergeant. He has jarred many students out of intellectual torpor, and the alumni love to tell stories about him. But there are some students who hate his guts. He has broken many a bruised reed and quenched many feebly smouldering fires. His method is many times effective, but not universally successful.

Then there is the methodical teacher. His lectures are perfect in their construction. His examinations come with clock-like regularity. The end of the subject is reached exactly at the end of the semester. The student at all times knows precisely what is expected of him and precisely where he stands. This man is an ideal teacher for the elect—those who have already become interested in the subject he teaches. To them he shows a thoroughness which is a complement for their enthusiasm. But it is doubtful if he can generate much enthusiasm when it does not exist.

Then there is the enthusiast. He has something that he is burning to impart. He forgets everything but his message. No method can constrain him. One of the high lights of my own college experience was a man like that. I did not agree with a single one of his ideas, but I can safely say that most of my waking time for two years was taken up with answering what can only be described by the trite term, *his challenge*. This man made no assignments; he forgot them in the rush of argument. He also usually forgot about examinations. And yet I never worked for any teacher as I did for him. But many students found him quite uninteresting.

The rambling teacher is a type often frowned upon by the methodologists. He can easily be distracted by red herrings dragged across the trail. He doesn't get to the end of the subject at the end of the semester. He is rather frequently imposed upon. But if he has something to say, many students will find his courses of supreme value. This is particularly true of those students who have no intention of becoming specialized scholars. In my case, I owe my conception of social justice to such a man and I would not trade it for any of the more systematically learned truths.

There is another type more rare than the preceding. I might call him the expert expositor—the man who in a moment's conversation with a student can comprehend his difficulty and with a sentence can shed more light on a probblem than most of us can contribute in a week. Because of his peculiar ability, he is likely to be very impatient with any imposed method, and also with any student who cannot immediately comprehend when the solution of his problem is briefly sketched.

All those types have their excellencies and their drawbacks. No one of them can hope to be successful in teaching all types of students. A college is fortunate if it possesses examples of each, and of all the other types too. And a college is wise if it does not try to force teachers of these various types into uniformity. Granted now that the student must have an initial desire to improve himself, granted that he must at all costs learn how to read and write and that the teachers whose services he has access to are of many different types, what should be his training in methods of study?

Since the process of learning and that of teaching are so personal, we must lay it down as a principle that in the teacher-learner relationship the method must always be subordinate to the persons. Every student should receive very serious training in study and in thinking, but that does not mean that each student should receive, or each teacher give, the same training. It would be ideal if each student could experience the way in which each teacher in the institution does his own studying, not that the student may become an expert in all these ways, but that he may ascertain which way works best for him. Even within the specialties, we must beware of making the accepted method supreme, for most of the people who happen, at any given time, to be studying a particular specialty, are not planning to be specialists in that field themselves.

Each student should have experience of advancing in knowledge by careful and methodical work, wherein no stone is left unturned, no evidence left neglected, no authority unused. He may not use that method again in his life, but it has proven very fruitful for many people. (One has only to read the theses of graduate students to see that it is not always so fruitful.) But he should also have opportunity to see how knowledge can be attained dialectically, by the brilliant play of mind in discussion and argument as in the Socratic Dialogues. Sometimes insights and understanding come in this way which would not have been found in hours of plodding study. Such a dialectical process can, however, easily degenerate into a "bull session."

We should also furnish our young people with experience in co-operative work with knowledge as its goal. As it is, they work together, for the common good, in preparing for the Junior Prom, but not in learning. A division of an assigned subject into fields, with a field assigned to each member of the group, each member mastering the literature in his field, and a final sharing of the knowledge gained as well as constant consultation to compare progress —this will give the student a conception of the strength of united effort that he can well carry into other activities. But he should also have the experience of "working up" a subject all on his own, with books as his materials and with a barest minimum of guidance. This is of greatest importance, for we wish him to keep on in his quest for knowledge after he leaves our college, and in most cases he will have to do it without the help of a teacher. Since libraries are pretty generally accessible, he ought to learn how to carry on a project with them as his sole reliance. The necessity of learning this is another reason why the course cannot be the sole means of education. But again we must put off until later the discussion of this most important problem.

An absolute necessity, for one who wishes to experience all the fruitful methods of study, is some opportunity for complete concentration. This is impossible with the college curriculum as it usually exists. The high school graduate comes to college and is immediately plunged into an unfamiliar environment where at least five fields of knowledge, all of them to some extent unfamiliar and each of them flourishing a system of concepts distinct in itself, are presented to him simultaneously. The freshman finds that the teachers of these fields of knowledge are more or less in competition with each other for his time and attention. The only way he can concentrate on one subject is to neglect the others, and if he does that all the teachers but one are on his neck. The whole set-up is calculated to produce bewilderment or, at the best, superficiality; and one or the other of these conditions often remains with the student until the day of graduation. The bewilderment and superficiality are not the fault of the student but of the system.

An experience of total concentration is necessary. The

student must know what it is to live with a subject—to study it all day, to talk about it constantly with others who are doing the like, to go to bed with it, to wake up with it. This is by no means the only experience he must have— diversity of attention is a valuable experience, too—but he *must* have it, for in his later life he must know how to throw his whole self into solving a problem. And he should have it early in his college career. Why not, fellow teachers, organize our college so that the incoming freshman may in his tender months be introduced to one thing at a time? Why do we persist in throwing the whole book at him on his first day? It is my belief that, if we really wish to initiate young people into the life of the intellect, the revision of our programs so as to allow an early experience of concentration is a step which is *next* to the most important that we must take. Now let us come to the *most* important step.

Collegiate institutions in this country have almost completely neglected what has in general human experience been found to be the most effective means of stimulating the mind of a person who is growing into maturity. It is this means which Cardinal Newman has in mind when he says that young men coming up to the University and living together for three years would be educated even if there were no teachers. If this statement seems absurd to us, it is only because we have not succeeded in developing a type of institution where the proper conditions exist. We have never built, in our colleges, a real community life—a community of learning. We have never tried to build our students into a community on the intellectual side. Their community has been social and athletic, but in things of the mind they have remained Robinson Crusoes. Neither have we tried to construct a community of students and teachers. The school's master-pupil relationship of the primary grades, with its natural antagonisms, sticks with us all through college. Neither have we brought about a community between teachers and adminstration. There we have the employer-employee relationship which has always been most productive of friction. And in our failure to build a genuine community life among all persons connected with our college, we are depriving our students of the very best means of learning, a means which transcends and makes effective all the methods of study that we can teach them, a means which can give them that initial inspiration that we spoke of earlier and can keep it glowing by continual refreshment.

In our medieval educational tradition, of which we speak so much and which we heed so little, it seems to have been recognized that when the student entered the university the birch rod was laid aside in favor of another principle of teaching. The student was initiated into the guild of learning, into a community whose reason for existence was a common interest in things of the mind. The life of the community was intellectual activity. Its members were people in various stages of acquiring knowledge. The neophyte was educated by being drawn into this intellectual life.

It would be a great triumph in educational technique if we could create in our Catholic colleges some such community of learning, and it is by no means impossible. The first essential is to break down our ideology according to which the standardized course, with its own credits and examinations, is the unit of education—indeed, it is to break down the idea that education is made up of units at all. We must substitute the idea that education is the growth of a human mind in knowledge and skill. Once we seize upon this truth, we can realize the further truth that minds that are progressing together can assist and stimulate each other and that minds that have progressed further can aid those who have not gone as far. When we have grasped these fundamentals, we can understand what a community of learning is—a community of people, all desirous of advancing along the road to truth, among whom subsist a complicated set of personal relationships and activities, which are all calculated to help in some way toward the goal.

In such a situation the complexion of the college would be quite different from what it is now. All the activities of learning, formal and informal, would be given respectable rating. The course would be only one of these, though perhaps, owing to our tradition, it would hold some place of honor. In addition to courses there would be many group projects carried on by students with the help of their elder brothers, the teachers. There would be students carrying on private projects on their own in the library. There would be groups getting together informally in the evening or at meal time for conversation and argument. The students, accustomed to toss ideas back and forth all through their college days, would find that these ideas had become their own, burned into their minds, and ready for use all through their lives. And behind all these activities there would be going on all the time the discipline of reading and writing, in addition to the constant discipline that comes from the meeting of minds.

To the incoming freshman the college would say, "You are now becoming a member of a kind of community new to you. Your best training will be to plunge into the life of this community and take part in its activities. Some of these activities will be required, some are optional. You should try to find the activity in which you learn best. From time to time the college will check up on you by examination, to see how you have progressed both in knowledge and skill. By the time of graduation you will be supposed to have mastered such and such skills and such and such subjects. Now get to work."

I am always impressed by the way in which our students make football the subject of informal group study. They live with it. It is the subject of their spare time conversation and arguments. The pressure of public interest draws even the lukewarm into it. The student body as a whole becomes expert in the field of the knowledge of the science and art of the pigskin—and this without any formal class work at all and entirely without benefit of any paid teaching staff. In some such way the community of learning—if we had it—could inspire and educate the students. When we see how subjects not on the curriculum are taken up with such gusto and learned so well and so thoroughly and so permanently, altogether apart from our efforts, we can realize how valuable an aid these efforts would have if the immense educative potential of the student community could be channelled in the same direction as our teaching is. This can be accomplished, and is being accomplished in some parts of the world, by the community of learning.

I am sure that many of us teachers long for a wider opportunity to become acquainted with our students. We are interested in their intellectual development as a whole, and not merely in that side of it which concerns the subject that we teach. The course system as it exists rather puts us in a straight jacket in our relation with the younger generation. It establishes a formal barrier. It walls up a narrow area in which we preside and suggests that it is none of our business what goes on outside that area. But since informal contact of young minds with older ones is for both one of the most fruitful methods of learning, this particularizing effect of the course system is disastrous for education. It is particularly disastrous now that we are coming to see the necessity of integration in knowledge.

The concept of integration assumes an acting agent, something that brings together in ordered arrangement what was disordered before. In knowledge it is the mind that integrates, just as it is the mind that learns. And the mind of the learner can best be helped in integrating its knowledge by the companionship of a mind that has already progressed further along the road of integration. But the companionship of the two minds, to be effective, must continue through all the fields of knowledge which have to be integrated. A course in philosophy cannot do it, although a philosopher can if he has opportunity to function outside his course. So can a scientist, or a mathematician, or a teacher of literature, provided each of these is something more than a specialist and is allowed to act outside his specialty.

Perhaps the chief reason for the great need of developing in our colleges a community of learning over and above the course and credit level is the fact that it gives a chance for teachers and students to associate in an atmosphere which makes it possible for the students to receive real aid in integrating their knowledge.

Here at the end of our discussion let us come back for a moment to those students whom we welcomed into our school earlier—the sow's ears which were to be made into fine leather wallets. In the give and take of the community they will perhaps not show such brilliant performance. Their examinations will not be the ones we mention when we are recounting our successes. Their essays will probably not be published. But they will be there, learning solidly and integrating what they learn. Because making solid Christians is one of the goals we have accepted—and this goal is of course for the scholars too—our community must be broader in its intention than was the community of the medieval university. The activities which we encourage must not be solely those of the speculative intellect. We must encourage also the manifold activity of the Christian apostolate and all the interests whose goal is the Christian reconstruction of the social order. All these activities and interests can be studied. But more than that, they can actually be practiced. The student who is outstanding in apostolic activity should not receive less recognition than the one outstanding in mathematics. This must be so because we have claimed that we produce good Christian leaders as well as scholars.

In the community of learning there will be a common fund of ideas studied, discussed, meditated on, and fought over. About these ideas there will be much difference of opinion. There will be arguments and intellectual factions. Leaders will have followings and opponents. Conflicts will be common, perhaps too common, and that on which all agree will be smaller than what one might suppose. Particularly with young people, the excitement of intellectual disagreement can be a real stimulant to thinking. A college should be generous rather than strict in allowing this, for to suppress it too much can result in stagnation. All this means that in our intellectual community it may be difficult to find much visible unity.

To balance the intensity of disagreement which is bound to rise in a group that makes thinking its chief activity, the teachers, as the elder brothers, will have to make an effort to prevent factionalism by teaching and practicing charity and understanding. Whatever bonds of comradeship and common interest exist must be constantly strengthened, so that the community may remain a unity. The centrifugal tendency of awakening thought will have to be met and overcome by a heightened experience of union. Therefore, those particular activities which our college performs as a part of the Mystical Body of Christ must never be treated in such a way that anyone could think for a moment that they were of secondary importance. No academic activity can be preferred to the work of God. And for minds awakening to the joy and the power of thought there must be a parallel awakening to an appreciation of that greatest work of thought and action: the worship of God. We the teachers, and our students with us, and whatever of the administration there will be remaining in a civilized college, all of us together will find our personal realization and our bond of corporate unity in an active, rational, and personal participation in the Divine Liturgy.

Here is the center of that life of common learning which we can offer to our young people as a setting wherein they can learn how to study.

Discipline and the Case Method

By Reverend Paul Hanly Furfey

The efficiency of instruction is improved if students are given an immediate opportunity to apply practically the knowledge they acquire in the classroom. It is this principle, of course, which justifies the laboratory method in chemistry, physics, and biology. It is this principle, too, which justifies field-work training for students of social service, clinical instruction for medical students, practice in the ward for student nurses, and the use of the moot court in the law school. The purpose of the present paper is to suggest that the principle could be applied still more widely and particularly that extracurricular activities can often be used for field training in various areas.

Some of the advantages of practice training can be explained by the well-known *law of effect,* which states that reward reinforces learning while punishment inhibits.[1] The student who applies his knowledge in the laboratory or in some sort of field work and finds success is rewarded with a consciousness of achievement. His learning is reinforced thereby. On the other hand, if his practice is unsuccessful, the failure itself is a sort of punishment. Incipient bad habits are broken down and he is stimulated to seek a modification of his methods.

Successful achievement can convince the learner of the value of his training; it can also build up his own self-confidence. A student in a class of creative writing may be only mildly interested in the subject; but if he submits an article to his college paper and has it accepted and published, his interest may be immediately heightened. He has a concrete proof that he is learning successfully. He begins to follow the teacher with closer attention. On the other hand, the cocksure student may argue at length with his teacher in class and hold tenaciously to his own opinions,

---

[1] This is a greatly oversimplified statement of the law of effect. The law involves a number of very complex problems. For a good critical review of work in this area, see, Leo Postman, "The History and Present Status of the Law of Effect," *Psychological Bulletin,* XLIV (1947), 489—563, where 332 titles are reviewed.

but he cannot argue with the facts. In the laboratory or in his field work he puts his personal theories to the test and he must abandon them if they fail. The student who meets failure in his practical training is learning humility the hard way.

Laboratory and field practice add realism to a subject. Chemical compounds are mere names in the classroom, but in the laboratory they are visible and tangible substances. The description of a certain disease may seem clear enough to the medical student from the textbook or the classroom lecture; but in the clinic, where the *casus typicus* is rare, he begins to learn the complexity of his subject. The student of social work may have fixed ideas about unmarried mothers; but when she begins to deal with actual unmarried mothers in her field work, she finds that her ideas need revision. A case may seem very simple to a law student; but when he argues it in the moot court, he begins to discover some aspects which he had overlooked. There is nothing like the give-and-take of actual practice to dispel false ideas and reinforce sound ones.

Practical training stimulates curiosity and provides the opportunity to make minor, personal discoveries. The social work student comes back from her field work full of questions. She turns to her supervisor eager for direction. Gradually, if she is a good student, she begins to develop minor modifications of method of her own, modifications which suit her own personality. If they work out well and are approved, she feels the thrill of a modest personal triumph. The student in training who discovers small problems and solves them for himself is getting an excellent preparation for serious research work.

In our colleges we reward and punish students somewhat artificially by the grading system. The good student is rewarded by high marks and perhaps by prizes and scholarships which are correlated with them. The poor student is punished by low marks, failures, and possibly by being dropped from the college rolls. Certainly a grading system of some sort is essential. If a college should discard grades altogether and graduate all students automatically after four years of residence, one fears that few would be idealistic enough to do their best work. A grading system is essential, but it is also necessarily somewhat artificial. It is a construct of educators. On the other hand, success or failure in actual practice is a system of natural rewards and punishments. This is not a construct of educators. Good or bad results are naturally and inherently connected with good or bad work. The student of creative writing whose manuscripts are accepted by editors knows that he is learning his subject; a high grade awarded by the teacher is merely confirmatory evidence. The college which provides its students with wide opportunities for practical experience is supplementing and reinforcing its grading system with a very effective system of natural rewards and punishments.

Opportunities for laboratory and field training are, for the most part, confined to the practical sciences. It would be hard to imagine a system of field training for a speculative science like metaphysics. Students in a course of ancient history can hardly find an opportunity to apply their knowledge practically. The attraction of such disciplines lies in the sheer joy of intellectual accomplishment, a knowledge and an insight which are their own reward. There remain, however, many subjects in the college curriculum which offer possibilities for immediate application. Without too much difficulty college administrators can provide opportunities for students to use the knowledge they have acquired.

As was stated above, this paper is not principally concerned with opportunities which may be provided within the curriculum itself. Laboratories and various sorts of field training are too universally accepted to need defense. Everyone admits that a course in chemistry or physics or biology without laboratory hours would be sadly incomplete. Modern language courses are increasingly using classroom practice in the actual use of the language. There is no need to re-emphasize once more the advantages of such procedures. Rather, the present paper is concerned with the possibility of using extracurricular activities and even extracollegiate activities for a similar purpose. The proposal is for a closer integration of these activities with the college curriculum. The total educational experience of the student in college should be regarded as a unit. There is no reason for making a very sharp distinction between that part of his education which is part of the formal curriculum and that part which is not.

Extracurricular clubs providing opportunities for oral practice in a foreign tongue are familiar supplements to modern language courses. Most of us are familiar with French circles, German clubs, and the like. Students conduct meetings, listen to lectures, or perhaps give a one-act play, all in the foreign language. A club of this sort can be a great help to the ambitious student because he can practice his new language in an atmosphere which is more natural than the classroom. The situation itself provides a stimulus for trying to speak and to understand. However, even the foreign language club itself has a certain element of artificiality. The most convincing test of one's proficiency in a foreign tongue is the ability to get along in an environment where that language alone is spoken. Foreign travel, therefore, deserves encouragement. The ordinary conducted tour, though valuable in other respects, is not usually very helpful for linguistic practice. There are, however, other possibilities. Many foreign universities welcome American students for their summer sessions and are willing to make special arrangements for them. Sometimes it is possible to arrange for a student to spend part of the summer living with a private family where a foreign language is spoken. To be alone in a non-English speaking environment is a situation which gives enormous scope to the law of effect. An inadequate knowledge of the language leads to all sorts of embarrassment and inconvenience, while each step forward in proficiency is rewarded immediately and convincingly.

College papers and magazines offer obvious opportunities for extracurricular training in journalism, creative writing, and art work. The possibilities in this field are familiar to administrators and do not call for much comment. If the college has a well-organized publicity office, it may offer some part-time paid jobs to students who thus gain valuable journalistic experience. Students should be encouraged also to write for newspapers and magazines of general circulation. Even to write a "letter to the editor" and have it published is an encouraging experience. Ambitious student writers should by all means learn to typewrite rapidly and accurately. If the college offers a course in typing, student writers should be encouraged to take it. Thus, once more, curricular and extracurricular activities are brought into relation.

Debating societies and oratorical contests are familiar means for offering students training in public speaking. In addition there are, of course, a good many miscellaneous occasions in college life which call for public speaking by a student, varying from a few words of introduction for a visiting lecturer to the formal valedictory at commencement. The ordinary meetings of college societies offer opportunities for speaking which must not be overlooked. The student who learns to express his point of view convincingly in a few words at a meeting certainly acquires valuable experience. All these opportunities give the student a chance to apply practically what he has learned in courses in public speaking and English composition; but they also give him a chance to apply what he has learned in various specific fields. For example, if he is debating some economic topic, he can apply what he has learned in his economics classes.

College dramatics are another extracurricular activity in which classroom knowledge can be practically used. If the college offers courses in dramatics, then of course the application is very immediate and obvious. But there are other applications as well. Students may present original one-act plays and practice what they have learned in creative writing courses. If they revive an Elizabethan play, they recall what they learned in historical courses in English literature. Possibly art students may use their special skills to design stage settings or paint scenery. Home economics students can help to plan and make costumes. The play itself may be chosen to express a particular point of view on some social question and when the choice is being made, students of the social sciences may be able to contribute valuable advice. The management of the business details connected with the play can give practical training to students in business courses. A college play can be managed as a thing apart with little relation to anything else that is going on in the institution; but on the other hand it can be used as a means of coördinating and applying practically the knowledge and skills imparted in a number of different teaching departments.

It is easy to multiply examples of the use of curricular

knowledge in extracurricular activities. The music department has an obvious outlet in the college glee club, the college orchestra, and the college choir, beside concerts and recitals that are wholly musical, there are all sorts of functions which call for some music as part of the program. Art students can make posters and perhaps design decorations for college affairs. The publication of a yearbook or the management of a large college function such as a junior prom involves a good many business details. In a large college substantial sums of money may have to be handled. This fact gives opportunity for practical training useful for students of business. Home economics students may have a hand in the management of the college cafeteria. The campus is a little world which reflects a great many of the activities of the big world outside. The resourceful college administrator can train students to apply on the campus the skills which they will apply on a larger scale in later life.

There is one specialized area of student activity which calls for more extended comment than the more standard types of extracurricular activities which have just been discussed. I have in mind what may be roughly classified as "Catholic Action," at least in the broad sense of that term. Activities of this sort are particularly helpful in that they provide students of the social sciences an opportunity to apply practically what they have learned. It is hard to teach efficiently and well any science which deals with social problems unless students gain some familiarity with such problems at first hand. A student can easily finish his sociology course with only a vague idealism which bears little relation to everyday life. Or he may develop his own personal and quite unrealistic theories about the reform of society. Even the excellent student with a sound theoretical grasp of social problems lacks something if he has never contributed any personal effort toward their solution. To be thoroughly educated he should be trained both in theory and in practice. Before graduation he should have had some realistic experience in social action.

Catholic Action in the stricter sense is probably most often represented in our colleges by groups which call themselves "Young Christian Students." The movement is still relatively young and relatively unstandardized; various groups have attained varying degrees of success. European experience has shown that the successful organization of such groups requires not only enthusiasm and patience, but also a high degree of specialized skill. In the United States the movement is making steady progress. Its leaders are learning by experience. The future is bright. The Young Christian Students attack social problems in a thoroughly realistic spirit. They are taught to study the problems of their own environment, to canvass systematically the various possible ways and means of meeting them, and to act only on the basis of this careful preliminary discussion. The members try to base their action consciously and explicitly on Catholic principles. This emphasis on the intellectual basis of social action makes it very easy to correlate the movement with classes in religion and sociology in which these principles are taught. Thus Young Christian Student groups offer a very natural means for practical training in the application of classroom knowledge.

There are a number of other student activities which may be classified as Catholic Action if the term is interpreted somewhat broadly. These include the work of groups organized to promote international peace, to improve interracial relations, to assist home and foreign missions, to give catechetical instruction, and to help in various other good works. Sometimes action of this sort may be carried on with little or no formal organization. Students as individuals can be encouraged to teach Sunday school in their own parishes or in other parishes which are short of teachers. As individuals they can try to convert non-Catholic friends, visit the sick in homes or hospitals, or collect money for the support of the poor. In fact, any of the corporal or spiritual works of mercy can be performed on an individual basis. The college should not try to monopolize all the time which the students give to social action. It is well to encourage them to join organizations outside the college itself so that their membership may persist after graduation. A certain college offers a course in Catholic Action and one of the requirements for passing the course is that each student give a specified number of hours of work to any of a number of approved Catholic organizations which are not connected with the college itself. The students benefit by contact with varied groups off the campus and they pool their experiences in classroom discussions.

It is easy to see how the various activities which have just been described can be correlated with college courses. For example, the student may learn in the classroom about the status of the American Negro and the discrimination from which he suffers. This theoretical knowledge is valuable in itself, but it becomes very much more valuable if it is applied. A college unit of the Catholic Interracial Council will provide the organization framework for changing attitudes toward Negroes on the campus itself. Volunteer social work in colored sections of the city will bring a first-hand knowledge of the problems which Negroes face. Friendships with individual Negroes and interviews with the local leaders of the race will be enlightening. By such varied activities students can gain a realistic knowledge of interracial problems which could never be gained in the classroom; at the same time classroom instruction will help them to interpret their first-hand contracts in the light of broader principles. Students whose understanding of race relations is both theoretical and practical can plan a program of social action realistically. They will not make the mistakes which well-intentioned enthusiasts too often make in this area.

Settlement houses are a useful means of bringing students into contact with the problems of deteriorated areas. Universities and colleges played a prominent part in the early history of the settlement house movement and the precedent is a good one. Most colleges would probably feel that for the college to sponsor a settlement house of its own would be too ambitious a project; but it should not be too difficult to arrange for a close working relationship between the college and some existing local settlement. Such a relationship can be mutually advantageous. The settlement profits from the interest and the volunteer work of the students. The students gain acceptance in the neighborhood through their connection with the settlement, and the settlement staff has the expert knowledge to answer their questions. Here in Washington a Catholic settlement, Fides House, has a close, though unofficial, connection with the Department of Sociology of the Catholic University, the director of the house being a member of the departmental teaching staff. The effort is made to apply Catholic principles very consciously in the work carried on and a considerable number of students have participated at various times.

Sodalities, third orders, and other pious societies are directly concerned with the spiritual perfection of the individual members; but the individual cannot grow in virtue without affecting his neighbors. The student who strives for perfection will grow in charity and will express his love for others by performing the spiritual and corporal works of mercy. He should realize, moreover, that his neighbor's welfare depends on the state of society in general. Therefore, the active member of a pious society who takes his duties seriously must logically be concerned with problems of social reconstruction. His obligations as a good Catholic demand no less than that. Of course, a pious society can easily lapse into mere formalism or it can promote a self-centered type of religiosity which involves little active interest in one's neighbor's welfare. But a pious society infused with the proper spirit is a center of active charity and its members are eager to promote any good work for the benefit of others. A pious society can thus be a means for translating the principles taught in the religion class into active works for the amelioration of the social conditions considered in the sociology class.

We have been considering various ways in which the student may apply his theoretical knowledge practically during his college course. It seems safe to assert that the ability to make such practical applications is an important mark of the educated man. The ideal of education should not be to turn out mere theorists or mere empiricists. The ideal should be to graduate students who have grasped the relation between theory and practice, who can translate abstract principles into feasible programs of action, who show the results of their education concretely in their own lives. A course in home economics should make good housewives. A course in sociology should make intelligent and active citizens. A course in literature should make enthusiastic lovers of good books. Education which does not concretely affect the lives of the students is inefficient and superficial education.

These facts pose a problem for us as educators. How should we rate the success of a student? Should our rating depend entirely on his ability to write a good examination paper or should we consider also his ability to apply his knowledge practically outside the classroom? The problem is already answered in some departments of instruction because the student is traditionally required to apply his knowledge in laboratory or fieldwork courses within the curriculum itself. The teacher of analytical chemistry demands that his students turn in good examination papers, but he also demands that they go to the laboratory and show their ability to make analyses; students must master both theory and practice to get a good grade. Similarly, the grades given a student of social work will depend both on success in the classroom and success in a fieldwork placement. However, there are other sciences in which grades are customarily assigned on the basis of classroom work exclusively and the student is not required to demonstrate his ability to make successful practical applications. Is this a mistake?

Let us consider a concrete example. Here are two students of sociology. The one is a brilliant student in the classroom. His examination papers show an excellent grasp of facts and principles. Yet outside the classroom he has no practical, active interest in social action of any sort. He appears to be wholly wrapped up in himself and he has no time to contribute to the welfare of others. The other student, on the contrary, shows only average ability in class; but what he does learn, he applies successfully. He is an enthusiastic member of a Catholic Action group. He gives his time generously as a volunteer in a settlement house. He is always ready to lend a hand in any worthy project for social action. Moreover, he shows sound, practical judgment in all these activities, the ability to distinguish between what is feasible and what is not feasible under a given set of circumstances. Which of these two students is the better sociologist? According to the traditional grading system, the first is easily superior. Yet is this judgment fair? Should not the application of knowledge be taken into account as well as the acquisition of knowledge? A factual appreciation of the nature of education would seem to require an affirmative answer.

It would seem reasonable to demand that students majoring in sociology should devote some time to social action of one sort or another either on or off the campus. Sociology itself is most often classified as a speculative science, but it is not desirable that the student's interest in society should remain entirely on the speculative level. Before graduation he should be required to prove that he can translate theory into practice. Sociology has been used here as an illustration; of course, the same principle applies to other sciences as well. Some sort of academic recognition should be given to students who can prove that they know how to apply their knowledge well. If a student of English publishes articles in magazines, if a student of business subjects gets a job in an office and does efficient work, these facts should be taken into consideration when grades and credits are being assigned.

The principles which we have been discussing imply that the teacher, as well as the student, should be expert in the application of the knowledge which he commands. If the teacher of creative writing is himself a successful author his students will have more confidence in him. A lawyer who has been successful in the courtroom has an advantage over the mere theorist as a teacher. A certain school of social work encourages teachers to take regular jobs in agencies during the summer vacation so that they may remain closely in touch with their field. A college should always be very willing to grant a leave of absence to a faculty member who wants to work in some practical undertaking related to his subject. His absence may cause temporary inconvenience, but he will be a better teacher in the long run.

The teacher who is in close touch with the practical applications of his subject can make his classes more vital. He always has actual examples at hand to illustrate his teaching. He is always realistic and he never makes impractical proposals. He may be widely read, but he is never merely bookish. In social sciences such as economics, politics, or sociology, this realism is particularly necessary. These fields are plagued by the presence of numerous conflicting theories which confuse the student. Cocksure propagandists are constantly offering their panaceas which have often been dreamed up with little consideration of the actual facts. A teacher needs to have his feet on the ground if he is to guide the student through this confusion. If a teacher has wide practical experience in the application of his knowledge he can be a safe guide. He will be in a position to show students convincingly what is feasible and what is not.

The ideal of education is to prepare students for life. We should not think of this as a vague goal to be realized at some indefinite time after graduation. It is an ideal whose realization should begin immediately. The student should start to apply his knowledge at once. If he can apply it well today in his campus life, then we can be confident that he will also apply it well after graduation. If he cannot profit by his knowledge now, he probably will never do so in the future. We should seize every opportunity to help the student to use his training practically while he is still in college. We should be willing to spend a good deal of time and thought in order to make this possible to him.

Discipline, Marks, Rewards, and Punishments

By Willis Dwight Nutting

The need for integration in knowledge has been realized by our educational institutions only in recent years. Our whole standardized way of doing things was built up when people were interested in other goals. This includes our way of teaching, the methods of study that we encourage, our discipline, our examinations, our penalties, and our standards of attainment. All these educational habits grew up, became common property, and finally became vested interests while people were completely unconcerned with the problem of putting together what they had so long been busily engaged in taking apart. It being true then that our whole mass of educational practice developed under the inspiration of an ideal in which integration played a minor role, it should not cause surprise if the adoption of the ideal of integration were to necessitate a revision in this practice so large as to take on some of the aspects of a revolution. I say this by way of explanation of the very real radicalism of some of the ideas expressed in this Workshop.

In no field will the revision be greater than in that of rewards and punishments. If there is an alteration in the goal there is bound to be an alteration in the system of sanctions by which the students are encouraged to attain it. There cannot escape being a change in what is required, what is encouraged, and what is forbidden.

The chief sanctions must, of course, remain the same, even though the attainments for which they are given and the failures for which they are withheld may be in some respects different. The most important reward given by the college will be the degree, the final stamp of the college's approval; and the most significant punishment will be the refusal of the degree. In like manner, the most significant sanctions prior to the final approval or disapproval will be, at the end of each semester or each year, the permission to continue on to the next part of the program or the withholding of this permission.

We will give essentially the same rewards and punishments, but that for which we give them or refuse to give them cannot be the same as it is today if we really expect our students to strive for integrated knowledge.

What is that for which the college shall give its rewards, both preliminary and final? We said in our former discussion that what our colleges promised to prospective students, and what parents expected, was that the boys and girls should make something of themselves, that they should be improved and made into something finer than they were before. I should think then that the chief thing that should win our approval ought to be the fact that the student actually has improved, that he is something better than he was when he came to us. I should think also that the college had the right and duty to specify certain kinds of attainment and certain degrees of attainment which the student must possess if he is to receive the final seal of approval. Further, it would seem justifiable for the college to set certain preliminary goals of attainment which the student must reach by certain specified times if he is to receive the preliminary reward which consists in permission to go on.

All this sounds rather obvious. It is. But the conclusions that follow from it are not so obvious. Indeed they would revolutionize our whole system of rating people.

What are the attainments for which we will reward our students? First, there is a certain *content* of knowledge that we may require in the final reckoning and in the preliminaries. We have a right and duty to make our requirements stiff enough so that the average person that comes to us will have to make serious effort in order to meet them. Secondly, we can require the attainment of certain rhetorical *skills*—the correct use of the language in speech and writing, the ability to reason logically, and the ability to read with understanding. And thirdly, we must require a progressive *integration* of the fields of knowledge studied. This will consist in a realization of the relation of the different fields to one another, an ability to use knowledge gained in various fields for the solution of some particular problem, an awareness of the theological and moral implications involved in the problems of each field, and the application of this knowledge to Christian life and society, etc.

If that for which we reward the student is the attainment of a certain content of knowledge, a certain skill, and a certain integration of what is known, what are the means whereby we know that the required attainment has been gained? The time-honored institution of examination can determine the content of knowledge gained *if* that examination is fair; if, that is, it is a serious and adequate effort to find out what the student knows and does not know. But most examinations given are not fair, and the student retaliates by being quite willing to be unfair in his answering of them. We cannot know how much a man knows of a subject by giving him a six-question test at the end of the semester, or by giving a six-question test every week or every day. The asking of a few questions with the assurance that "if he knows any thing he will know this" is not true to what goes on in the human mind. The lacunae in anyone's knowledge occur in surprising places, as do the "filled-in spots" in a knowledge rather bare. Therefore, a man may know considerable without being able to answer any of the six questions, and he may be able to answer them all without knowing much else.

If we require effort on the part of the student in the attaining of knowledge, we must be equally serious in our effort to find out what he knows. The approval or disapproval of a man's accomplishment is a matter of vital importance to him, and must be to us also. Therefore, examinations which "count," those, that is, upon which our giving or withholding of approval is based, must be very searching. Since we are all pressed for time, it would be better to have these examinations fewer and longer, so that each one may be more adequate. The best way to find out what a man really knows is through a long and deliberate oral examination. I say that examinations which are to *count* must be searching. This does not preclude the possibility of more frequent short tests for the purpose of letting the teacher know how the student is progressing or for the purpose of spurring the student on. But unless they are honestly adequate for finding out the real state of affairs with regard to his knowledge, we cannot use them in marking.

We frequently hear of the impossibility of a quantitative standard in rating such an immaterial thing as knowledge. In one meaning of the term "quantitative standard" the criticism seems to be unjustified. How is it any worse, for instance, for me to say that a student got 85 than it is to say that he got B, or that he is high average. These are all ways of saying what I think of him on the basis of his accomplishment, and if I wish to express my estimation of him in percentages, that is no more materialistic than to express it by letters of the alphabet.

But there is a quantitative measurement that is pernicious, for it is the very negation of what we are trying to do. This is our system by which we regard knowledge as consisting of a certain number of units which can be added up and averaged, shifted around and transferred so that so much of this is equivalent to so much of that. This is the system of measuring attainment by credits. It is a carry-over from the ideology of industry. It regards the student as the Ford car on the assembly line, and the teacher as the mechanic who affixes parts on him, the part being the passed course. When he has acquired the correct number of parts, he is educated.

This, rather than marking by percentages, indicates the truly materialistic, quantitative view of knowledge. By it we regard knowledge as the sum-total of so many hours of work. But knowledge is not work. It cannot be measured by hours spent in its acquisition. And when we add up the credits of the courses passed, we are measuring something else than knowledge.

Let us remember what examinations are for. They are to indicate the state of a student's knowledge at the time they are given. They are not to supply a set of numbers whereby we can estimate his final attainment. We give examinations at the end of the first year to find out what our students know *at that time* and thus to determine whether they can go on to the next year's work. Once that has been done, the examination has performed its function. Its results had better be buried. To save these results, these marks, along with the marks of examinations at the end of other periods and to use them to help determine the standing of the student at the end of his college career is a practice which is altogether irrelevant to knowledge. At the end of four years we demand that the student show certain attainments. If he shows them by an examination, he has done what we require. Whether he did better or worse in former examinations can be of no consequence with regard to his attainment now.

The temptation to mark for work instead of for knowledge is always with us. It is a by-product of the point of view which regards an education as consisting of a series of units which can be added up. But if we proclaim a man as educated because he has, through a period of four years, fulfilled certain requirements as they came due, we are marking him for what he has done, not for what he is. We are rewarding him for work, not for knowledge. But such practice is completely contrary to the whole *rationale* of academic reward. We should reward a man with a degree as a sign of our approval that he has attained a certain degree of knowledge. We should give him a degree because he knows, not because he once knew. Suppose our subject is history, a certain knowledge of which we consider necessary for an educated man. Can we, consistently with the true significance of a degree, give a degree because a man has certain credits in history? Certainly not, for credits in history mean only that he once knew history. But we can only give our approval of him as an educated man if he knows it now. If he took history in his freshman year, wrote a good examination and passed, the fact that we let him go on is his reward for that attainment. He has no more rewards coming for that. The degree is the reward for what he knows on the completion of his college course, not for what he knew once upon a time and may well have forgotten. And what he knows now can be ascertained by a thorough, honest, adequate comprehensive examination now. Ladies and gentlemen, our system of giving rewards based on averages or on past accomplishment is contrary to the whole meaning of education.

But now I hear a chorus of objections. "How can you expect a student to remember at the end of his senior year the history that he learned his first year in college?" To this I can reply that throughout most of the world just this *is* expected of the student. One of the great differences between the European and American systems of education is the circumstance that in Europe it is assumed that if a student has "been over" a certain subject he will remember it, while in America it is assumed that he will not. The difference is not in the intelligence of the two students, I am sure, but in the way the two learn. This brings us back to a subject discussed in my former paper: the community of learning.

Because neither we nor the students can do everything at once, teaching and learning must take place step by step. If the college course lasts four years, some of the teaching and learning must be done in the first year, a long time before graduation. But these steps in teaching and learning cannot be things that have any sufficiency in themselves. They have significance only as means of improving a mind. They are completely ancillary and nothing more. The condition of the mind, as improved by them, is the only thing that can rationally "count" in our estimate of the success or failure of a student's college career.

The history course in the student's first year, if it has meaning at all, gives him some insights which remain with him forever and which aid him in his further accumulation of knowledge and wisdom. At the time of his graduation, when we are ascertaining whether or not we are going to bestow our approval upon him, one of the things we wish to find out is the status of his historical knowledge *at that time*. The fact that he once knew it is irrelevant. If what he learned in his freshman year has not remained with him, we should give him zero in history.

This seems a very harsh saying and contrary to the realities of the situation. It is, however, quite in line with a correct educational ideal. Can the realities of the situation be made to correspond with the ideal? Not as long as we maintain our practice of holding the course as the exclusive medium of teaching and learning, for the course, with its credits on the permanent record, is a self-sufficient unit. The credit given for it when it is "passed" means that the work done in it will "count" even though the knowledge gained by this work is completely forgotten. There is nothing in the regime, of course, to encourage the further activating of the ideas gained in the course. As a matter of fact it might even seem advantageous to the student to forget what he has learned in former courses so that he can clear his mind for concentration on the courses he is taking now.

The only rational function of a course is that of either launching a person on a new line of thought by giving him some principles, some inspiration, and some information, or else continuing him with greater facility on a line of thought upon which he has already embarked. The course is a means of initiation and additional stimulation. Neither a course nor the totality of courses taken together can supply an environment for the maturation of knowledge and its integration. This function can only be performed by the community of learning.

In the course the student receives the equipment for the community life. Thus equipped, he plunges into the life of the community. The ideas and the information gained in the course are exercised here, the ideas being sharpened and the information increased and burned into the memory by being kept constantly in use. When what is learned in the course is employed in countless situations and on innumerable occasions in the give and take of an alert community of learning, it becomes genuinely a part of the student's mind and is not forgotten. Our student of history will have better command of historical knowledge at his graduation than he had in his freshman year, even though he has not taken a course in history since that year; for he has had to use his historical knowledge in argument, he has had to view other knowledge in terms of its history, and he has had to use history as a means of integrating information that he has acquired. Under these conditions he should be able to pass a better examination on it at the end of his senior year than he could when he was "taking" a course in it.

We have been discussing the preliminary and final examinations for ascertaining whether or not the student has gained the content of knowledge that we expect of him. But we have had occasion also to speak of another attainment that he must reach: the integration of that knowledge. The very fact that a student will be expected to know, at the end of his four years, what he has learned during the whole period will mean that he will have to do some integrating. Our history student, for instance, will have had to integrate the content of whatever courses of history he may have had and he will have had to place the other knowledge he has acquired in its historical framework. Knowledge which has been maintained and used over a period of time cannot help becoming more or less integrated with other knowledge. Thus the final examination in any subject will reveal in some way the success that the student has had in integration.

It may be, then, that final examinations in the content of knowledge may be so constructed as to reveal to some extent the integration that has taken place in the mind of the student; but there will remain another kind of integration that must be ascertained before the degree is given. Since in our propaganda we claim that going to a Catholic college will fit a man for Christian leadership, we must make some effort to determine whether our candidates for the degree have any such fitness. We must expect them to show evidence of having appreciated the relation of their studies to Christian living and to the apostolate. This means an integration of what they have learned with what they are obliged to do. If the life of the community of learning is broadened, as it must be, to include both the study and the carrying out of the apostolate, the students will have much experience in this kind of integration, and they should have opportunity to reveal this experience in a final examination along with their revealing of the other things they have learned.

I must emphasize again that this insistence that Christian leadership is a goal of college education is not a dilution of a high ideal, not a mere subterfuge to disguise incompetence. It is itself the expression of a high ideal, and an ideal which appeals to Christian parents. It is because of this ideal that people send their children to us, and if we minimize it we are breaking faith with them. It is largely because of this ideal that those young people who have no predilection for specialized scholarship can attain positions of dignity and respect in the college community; for if the scholarly ideal were the only one recognized, they would be doomed to perpetually subordinate places. The leather wallet must have equal dignity with the silk purse.

The necessity of final examinations both in content and in integration of knowledge means that examinations must be to some extent divorced from courses. Even in the preliminary examinations, those which are intended to ascertain progress in integration would have to transcend the particular courses in which fields of knowledge were taught. And the final examinations, which are absolutely necessary if a man is to be judged by what he has come to be as a result of his years in college, cannot be simply parts of the courses taken in the last semester, for they will have to cover knowledge gained and integration made during the whole four years. The examination unattached to any course would also give the student opportunity to show what he had learned outside of courses, by participation in the life of the community of learning. It would thus allow all his knowledge to "count," whatever method of study it was gained by, and would be the most complete and honest way to find out what he really knows, and whether or not he deserves to receive the highest reward the college can bestow upon him: the degree.

Up to this point we have been discussing only the rewards and punishments given officially by the college. But running parallel to these there is a series of informal, unofficial sanctions which often has greater efficacy in determining the course of action of the student. The greatest of these informal sanctions is student public opinion. Sometimes this public opinion runs almost opposite in its effect to the official opinion of the school. We see this commonly in the persistence with which student public opinion plays up the athlete and plays down the "brain." It appears again in the common situation where the student is supposed to put up resistance against being taught and where he is practically ostracized if he appears eager to cooperate with the teacher in learning. All this is perhaps merely evidence of juvenility in the student body; but since the juvenility lasts into the senior year, it would seem to indicate that our students do not mature very well under our regime. An indication of something much more sinister, however, occurs where student public opinion practically forces the student to be an accessary in cheating.

We have all of us been exasperated at this tendency of student opinion to burn what we worship and worship what we burn, but we have perhaps not realized that we are partially responsible for it. We have not yet waked up to the fact that by perpetuating into college teaching the schoolboy-schoolmaster relationship of the primary grades, we have also perpetuated the natural corollary of that relationship: the schoolboy's idea that the schoolmaster is his "natural enemy" who is to be circumvented and bamboozled at every opportunity. If we can establish the more mature relationship in which the teacher appears as the adviser and elder brother of the young person who, though a beginner, is still a fellow member of the same craft, then perhaps we could hope for a student public opinion which would aid us in bringing about what we desire, namely, the acceptance by the student of the goal that we have marked out for him. Such relationship between teacher and learner can be developed in that community of learning about which we have talked so much. In such a community not only would the great educative energy of the student body help us in our task of teaching, but the great force of student public opinion would also push students on in their desire to learn and would reward their learning with its approval. It may be that our whole system of college education will stand or fall according as we succeed or fail in bringing the sanction of student public opinion in line with the sanctions that we impose officially. It may be only by success in this matter that we can obtain a flowering of intellectual and moral life which is commensurate with the latent potentialities of our American Catholic students.

There are still other rewards of informal character to be bestowed on excellence. These are friendships—friendships between students and teachers and friendships between students working together in the same field of study. Such things perhaps cannot be offered as an incentive to the student who is not doing as well as he should, for they can be appreciated only when enjoyed; but for the ones who enjoy them there can be no finer reward. A comradeship based on hard work together, in struggling with a problem and on a shared joy in its solution, is a satisfaction which the uninitiated know nothing about. So also is the comradeship of apostolic activity and of common liturgical worship. These things are the "over and above" blessings which college life can offer to its really good students. They are not mentioned in the catalogue nor do they figure in Commencement exercises, but they are the very best reward that a student can hope for. They last long after college days are past and they are a constant stimulation to further thought and work. A college which does not make such rewards possible for its people is cheating them out of their birthright. It is withholding the best from the best. And a college whose horizon extends no further than the course system will find that its students have very poor opportunity to engage in the activities which give rise to intellectual comradeships either between students or between teachers and students. It is in the community of learning, where much teaching and learning are done outside the boundaries of courses, that friendships based on common intellectual effort have best chance to flourish.

We have not yet discussed one of the attainments which we demand of the student before we bestow the degree upon him. This is a certain standard in skills. The increase in whatever skills we demand should be measured from time to time by examination, and the student should not be allowed to go on until he shows evidence of possessing the degree of proficiency required at any given time. Because of the lack of training in the fundamental rhetorical skills shown by most of our students, these examinations will have to be thorough and our requirements rigidly enforced. There is no field where attainment is more valuable than in the field of reading and writing. If we are to send forth educated people, we cannot let anyone slip through who cannot read and write—*really* read and write, that is.

But in these skills as in the other requirements that we impose, we dare not rest content with adding up marks and passing a student who has an average above seventy. That a student could spell and could write a passable composition and could read a book in his freshman year is a worthy accomplishment. It enables him to pass on to his sophomore year. But to graduate he must be able to spell and to write and to read a book in his senior year, which is another thing. If a man has lost in the intervening years the skill he had as a freshman, that is a catastrophe serious enough to justify our withholding his degree. It would not have happened if he had been required to use this skill constantly and to improve it all the time. There must be no let-up in our student's reading and writing and speaking and arguing. If he does not go out from us an articulate man, his knowledge will be of small use to him or to society.

In determining the final standing of the student at the end of his senior year, the college will have to decide what weight to give to content of knowledge, what to skill, and what to integration. These are all parts of the whole of knowledge, but they must be evaluated separately and each school will have its own scale of evaluation. But in giving the final reward of the degree, we are saying to the world, "Here is an educated person." Therefore, we will have to take care lest we give too great a value to one of the elements of knowledge at the expense of the others. We do not want to pass off as an educated man a mere rhetorician who has all the skills of expression but nothing to express. Neither do we wish to turn out a specialist who has no interest outside his field. And also we should be unwilling to put our mark of approval on a person who knows all the answers but does not know the questions, a person who has all the assurance in the world that he has made a successful integration and yet in reality is quite innocent of what has to be integrated.

The temptation to make a much too facile integration is the great danger, I believe, that lies in our path as we aim at integration in our Catholic college education. We are so justly confident that we are right that we are inclined to believe that we see more clearly than we actually do see, that we have the answers to problems that we do not understand any too clearly. If we are to be taken seriously, if we are to give our students an integrated knowledge that will stand up under criticism, we must not yield to this temptation. We must insist that our students have a solid knowledge of the fields they hope to integrate and of the ethical problems that they hope to solve by integrating their knowledge with their Christian living. And we teachers must be always on the watch lest we slide over difficulties in our great aim of building into one grand unity our knowledge, our Faith, and our life.

Discipline and the Realization of its Necessity

By Sister M. Honora

Catholic college education is perfectly frank about its desire to form students. It aims openly to make them other than they are when they come to it, not by the cookie-cutter methods with which modern educators credit it, but by the simple, yet difficult, process of inducing them to form habits of mind and will appropriate, first, to their rational creaturehood; then to their privileged status as sons of God. In other words, it subjects them to the discipline of truth. Since its basic objectives are certain and well-defined, the youth who are graduated from Catholic schools should be characterized by a readily discernible tendency: to think; to think with the Church; to act in accordance with their thinking. The actual *Catholicity* of the education we offer is, moreover, the determining factor in the degree of formation we succeed in effecting.

There are three major types of control in education today: the proponents of two of them know what they want taught and why; the leaders of the other are preoccupied with what they do not want because they cannot agree on what they do want and why. The first two approach relatively well their ideal of formation which is achieved by the integration of the whole person in the light of a single concept: the nature of man. The atheistic ideal starts in error and ends in evil, but its self-consistency results in a very real and lasting formation of its subjects. The Christian ideal starts with truth and ends with the good; its self-consistency, too, results in real and lasting formation. Schools that serve an atheistic state operate under pressure and surveillance to produce Communists, Nazis, or some other of the brood; Christian schools are subject to but one force—truth—and they operate to turn out men. The battle of the ages has always been between the two "formed" armies and it will be waged until the end of time. St. Augustine's *City of God* and St. Ignatius' meditation on the two kingdoms picture the struggle in the arena in which it initially takes place—the soul of the individual who has to resolve for himself in some fashion the tension of trying to be a responsible member of human society and still to keep what is God's out of the hands of Caesar.

The educational "masses" fail in the third group. Their numbers are largest in the United States because a democratic form of government is kinder than others to clouded objectives, hazy ideals, vacillating motives, unhampered experimentation. They are shepherded toward "the good life," now practically synonymous with "the goods of life," by leaders whose single point of unanimous agreement is the determination to keep God from interfering with the public schools. With God goes ultimate truth, of course, and, therefore, intellectual and moral stability. There are busy conferences about educating the whole student, integrating personality, and intergroup, intercultural, interracial, interfaith relations; the while a state-financed relativistic philosophy of education, of its nature variable and inconsistent, produces a horde of unformed factualists who live by expediency, a life only briefly predictable.

The formation of students in a Catholic college is not a matter of trial and error. Intellectual integration demands two things: a standard by which value can be estimated and the systematic use of the standard. In setting up a working plan that will incorporate these essentials, the Catholic educator has an inexhaustible treasure of wisdom and experience to draw upon: no less than the total deposit of Divine Revelation, husbanded and protected by the Church, expounded and channeled to men by the inextinguishable voice of Peter. Since teaching is the divinely assigned apostolate of the Church, the education of her children has always been a precious prerogative; of late years she has given particular attention to the problems of higher education in the light of world conditions.

In *Aeterni Patris,* a directive on Catholic education, Leo XIII speaks both in the line of a great tradition and in virtue of an immediate need—the dearth, at the end of the nineteenth century, of thinkers of one true mind. The time demanded a philosophy that would stabilize resistance to error and that would enable men to move forward intellectually with security of soul.

The Supreme Pontiff did not misconceive either the importance of philosophy or its efficacy. He had before him when he wrote the bitter strife of his day and the troubles that vexed public and private life, one cause of which he declared was "false conclusions concerning divine and human things" originating in the schools of philosophy:

> For since it is in the very nature of man to follow the guide of reason in his actions, if his intellect sins at all, his will soon follows; and thus it happens that looseness of intellectual opinion influences human actions and perverts them. Whereas on the other hand, if men be of sound mind and take their stand on true and solid principles, there will result a vast amount of benefits for the public and private good. We do not, indeed, attribute such force and authority to philosophy as to esteem it equal to the task of combating and rooting out all errors; . . . but the natural helps with which the grace of the divine wisdom . . . has supplied the human race are neither to be despised nor neglected, chief among which is evidently the right use of philosophy.[1]

There is a philosophy, the Pope points out in detail, which rightly used will furnish the universal natural basis without which "faith cannot shine, or walk, or grow," and it is this, the Thomistic system, behind which he puts the force of his authority. He is clear and emphatic:

> While We hold that every word of wisdom, every useful thing by whomsoever discovered or planned, ought to be received with a willing and grateful mind, We exhort you, Venerable Brethren, in all earnestness, to restore the golden wisdom of St. Thomas, and to spread it far and wide for the defense and beauty of the Catholic faith, for the good of society, and for the advantage of all the sciences.[2]

"Let carefully selected teachers," he further enjoins, "endeavor to implant the doctrine of Thomas Aquinas in the minds of students." [3]

Implanting the doctrine of Thomas Aquinas is no casual task; it is precisely the fundamental step in the formation of thinking men and thinking Catholics. Every curriculum in a college should embody a pattern of courses in philosophy and theology that will give the student a synthesis of truth, "a body of directive ideas forming a whole, and capable, like the magnet, of attracting and

---

[1] *Great Encyclical Letters of Pope Leo XIII* (New York: Benziger Brothers, 1903), pp. 35-36.
[2] *Ibid.*, p. 56.
[3] *Ibid.*

subordinating to itself all (his) knowledge."[4] This system of thought is the first step toward integration, the frame of reference by which he can evaluate new ideas and establish them in their proper place in the realm of wisdom and the hierarchy of temporal and eternal values. Random courses which supply only a juxtaposition of individual truths do not serve this purpose; instead of offering a basis for co-ordinating knowledge, they increase the already common enough impression that Scholasticism has nothing to say to the modern world. What Leo XIII had in mind was certainly the assimilation of the doctrines of Thomism, as Sertillanges says, for "their own intrinsic worth, and what is more and *more than anything*, for their adaption to the present time."[5] He specified that the "doctrine of Thomas be drawn from his own fountains, or at least from those rivulets which, derived from the very fount, have thus far flowed, according to the established agreement of learned men, pure and clear...."[6] Moreover, he initiated at Louvain a program of neo-Thomistic studies which would also make "this rich intellectual capital bear fruit in abundance" for the days we live in.

The method of the philosophy class should aim at two things: the revealing of the inherent fascination and the inviolable nature of truth; the stimulation of the student to the personal analysis, interpretation, evaluation, assimilation, and organization of philosophic knowledge, to the end that he will be impelled to use it. Memorization is a necessary discipline at any level of learning, but the philosophy teacher that permits students just to memorize is materially interfering with the intellectual development that should be the result not only of this but of their other courses as well. How can they *use* unassimilated lumps of theory that float around for a while on the surface of consciousness and then sink to a subconscious limbo probably never to be resurrected? The study of St. Thomas should result in an experimental appreciation of "that ready and close coherence of cause and effect, that order and array as of a disciplined army in battle, those clear definitions and distinctions, that strength of argument and those keen discus-

---

[4] A. D. Sertillanges, *The Intellectual Life;* tr. by Mary Ryan (Westminster, Md.: The Newman Press, 1948), p. 86.
[5] *Ibid.*, p. 87.
[6] Encyclical, *Aeterni Patris, Great Encyclical Letters of Pope Leo XIII*, p. 56.

sions, by which light is distinguished from darkness, the true from the false. . . ." [7]

Admittedly, the most effective discipline, and the only one that persists throughout life, is self-discipline; the best motivation for it is the desire to get at truth. Now we do not make truth; truth makes us. First, it perfects the intellect through the speculative virtues; then, in the well-schooled individual, it directs action—the making and doing of things. The person who does the truth in charity is the integrated man.

The road to truth is a two-way thoroughfare, hence the college is not alone a school of philosophy. The lamp of wisdom is fed by the exploration of any and all sources of knowledge; new learning is, in turn, lighted up by wisdom already acquired. If your souls (said Pius XII to the members of the Papal Academy of Sciences) would long for and look for truth, you will find it bound up in everything we see, hear, smell, taste, touch, and feel in thousands of forms, pursuing our intellect with the complexities of weight, number, measures, of visible and invisible motion, where it moves, transforms itself, shows and hides to appear close or farther away, where it defies our acumen, our machines, our experiments, and often threatens us with the terror of strength beyond our instruments, our devices—marvelous portents of our hand and industrious art. Such is the vigor, the appeal, the beauty, and the intangible life of truth which is set free by the aspect and by the investigation of the immense reality that surrounds us.[8]

There is no mistaking here the voice of the guide who will aid us to interpret the world, *our* world; it is he who watches upon the towers of the Church, exercising a living and unbroken magistracy. And he it is who can inspire our students to achieve as perfectly as they may "an absolute allegiance to eternal reality and a diligent attention to the things of time." [9]

There is still more than a trace in Catholic college circles of the conflict between the thought of those who, in their

---

[7] *Ibid.*, p. 47-48; cf. also "Pope Leo XIII and Modern Studies," *Dublin Review*, LXXXVI (January, 1880), 190-210.

[8] Address, *Al gradimento*, December 3, 1939, *Discorsi e Radiomessaggi di Sua Santita Pio XII* (Milano, Vita e Pensiero, 1941) 1, 401.

[9] Jacques Maritain, "Catholic Thought and Its Mission," *Thought*, IV (March, 1930), 537.

eagerness to sympathize with their age, in their haste to attain practical results "tend to forget that the prime requisites of all practical efficiency belong to the realm of the spirit"; and of the others who "under pretext of fidelity to the eternal," cling to fragments of the past, and not understanding the work of man, evidence "a kind of disdain for the Spirit which moves upon the waters, which renews the face of the earth." [10] Students sense the opposition between the two attitudes and will tend to idealize, and "extremize," one or the other unless they can be lifted into an atmosphere where truth is not confined to departments but penetrates every cranny of human interest and endeavor. This intellectual roominess exists only in the teaching of the Church.

What we often teach in our classrooms is what we think the mind of the Church ought to be, if it is still Catholic. A fresher approach, and one less liable to suffer from inevitable personal limitations, would be to open up to students in all departments the immediate sources of Catholic doctrine, particularly the papal documents. These are pre-eminent demonstrations of the application of eternally sound principles to contemporary problems, for the popes do give "diligent attention to the things of time."

Unfortunately, papal documents are unfamiliar territory to the great majority of teachers in Catholic colleges. The texts of several major encyclicals are used in social science courses on some campuses and in a few places other documents are introduced, but the light of the Church, so far as its contemporary expression to contemporary Catholics is concerned, certainly does not "shine to all that are in the house." Yet these statements are authoritative sources of information and direction and could play a tremendously effective role in molding the minds of students.

The supreme effort of the Papacy for the last seventy years has been to bring truth into the market place. For a century or more preceding Leo XIII, one encyclical after another took up the defense of the spirit against the inroads of a materialism that was invading progressively every phase of human life. With his pontificate began the urgent presentation of Christian principles in their immediate applicability to the problems growing inevitably out of the

---

[10] *Ibid.*, p. 535.

false philosophies rampant throughout the civilized world. Religious doctrine and practice have been presented, explained, and developed in the light of individual and social exigencies, and a pentecostal renewal of life has been proffered to all the works of man. "To find such an efflorescence of scientific thought, of scholarship and teaching joined to spiritual claims, on the very points where materialism and positivism had launched their most destructive attacks," says Count dalla Torre, "one must go back to the golden age of mediaeval learning . . . the age, let us never forget, when the triumph of the spirit reached its zenith." [11] A most extraordinary service would, therefore, be rendered to souls, to the Church, and to society, if Catholic colleges could animate their students "to study, interpret, and apply all the doctrines contained in the Papal decrees—not an isolated principle here and there, selected according to personal preference, but the pontifical documents in their entirety." [12]

Each pope elected is a man of his time. What is more, he is chosen by an international assembly of the keenest, most informed minds of the moment, to govern a supranational organization that literally reaches from end to end of the universe. Further, immediately upon his elevation his voice takes on the accents of the Living Christ. Even if, then, the aim of our education were merely to teach students *what* to think, his pronouncements should be at least as significant as those that are hourly prattled over the radio and headlined in the press. If it professes to teach them *how* to think, if by its very existence it reiterates: "Let this mind be in you, which was also in Christ Jesus," it can scarcely afford to neglect so rich a source of vital material.

What have the popes written about? Maritain's summary is sufficiently inclusive:

> Whether there be question of the major errors which afflict our age: Rationalism, Liberalism, Naturalism, Modernism; of the harmonizing of Faith with reason, of Divine wisdom with human knowledge; whether we concern ourselves with the world-wide expansion of the Kingdom of God, embracing all nations and races, or with the return of dissident sects to religious unity, or with the true notion

---

[11] Count dalla Torre, "The Crisis of the Spirit," *Catholic Mind*, XLII (February, 1944), 110.
[12] Maritain, *op. cit.*, p. 538.

of culture, of man's dignity, of human liberty; whether we treat of the problem of marriage and family life, of children's education, of civil society, of the origin of authority, of obedience to law, of the political evolution of modern institutions, of peace between nations and its necessary bases, of the Kingship of Christ over all peoples, of the condition of the working man, of private property, or interest and usury, of the living wage, of strikes and labor unions; in general, wherever there is question of the relationship of politics and economics with the Gospel and morals—we have at our command a vast and continually augmenting treasure of instruction.[13]

For the four pontificates preceding Pius XII, the encyclicals alone number 144; the documents of Pius XII, including 16 encyclicals issued up to March, 1950 and all other types of pronouncements recorded in print, are now past 1,300.[14] Granting that a definite proportion of this total are necessarily concerned with strictly ecclesiastical business, an amazing number treat of the day-by-day problems of the life·in us and around us: the questions that face the woman in the home, the man on the street, the doctor in his office; the judge, the legislator, the executive, the statesman; the things that bombard our eyes and ears and minds through print, radio, screen, and television. All of these penetrate within the confines of the college campus and must be met, directly or indirectly, in anticipation or by immediate solution; so if papal teaching is to make any noticeable contribution to the way they are met, it also has somehow to penetrate the campus—and permeate it.

It is not enough that principles be taught in certain courses in certain departments and left there. A principle unapplied is as useless as the talent that the man "digged into the earth and buried." Moreover, it is not merely the students in certain courses that need working truth. Granted, for instance, that those enrolled in sociology and economics know something about unions, what of the girl who cannot pay her tuition because of the coal strike; or the student whose father goes bankrupt in a small automotive accessories business because automobile workers have walked out, or the boy who will lose a necessary part-

---

[13] *Ibid.*, pp. 537-38.
[14] Sister M. Claudia, *Guide to the Encyclicals* (1878-1937) (New York: The H. W. Wilson Company, 1939), and *Guide to the Documents of Pius XII* (Westminster, Md.: The Newman Press, 1950).

time job unless he joins a union unscrupulously organized, or the groups that are taunted with the accusation that the Catholic Church is just for the wealthy, favors only capitalistic enterprise?

It is not that Pius XII can tell the miners to go back to work because they are upsetting people's minds, homes, and businesses, or that he will advise them to stick it out, no matter what; but he and his predecessors have pointed out repeatedly and illustrated amply the considerations that should determine individual and social thought and action in the field of organized labor. In a Catholic college, these considerations should be so disseminated that they will reach all students. Such dissemination implies that they are familiar to the entire staff: teachers, counselors, placement director, social action director, librarians, administration; that they can be and are explained, when opportunity offers, in class or out, objectively and sympathetically; that they are promoted among students, alumni, and community groups as the basis for the correction of contemporary evils in the field of labor relations; that they are consistently lived up to on the campus.

Illustrations could be multiplied almost beyond count of specific and general questions that demand a common understanding if the Catholicity of education is to mean anything substantial. Sporadic instruction may fortunately take root in individual minds, but to produce an active consciousness of a living body of truth, every element in the total of the tangibles and intangibles of campus organization, policies, teaching, learning, and action, must be marshalled to make its proportionate contribution to the definite cast we want to impart to the thinking and living of our students.

Hard work always stands between theory and accomplishment, and the situation here is no exception. The first step toward campus unity-of-thought is to convince the faculty that the literature of papal pronouncements touches every field, even though it is more extensive in some than in others. The next thing is to get them to catch up on what they have missed and to keep up with documents as they are issued. They will be agreeably surprised at the variety and timeliness of topics that the Sovereign Pontiffs deem worth attention, and inspired by the vision with which they treat them. They will be struck by the characteristic personal turn to even the formal approach of the encyclicals and, when working with contemporary documents, they will be delighted by the warm personal presence of Pius XII in everything he writes. Finally, each person on the staff, regardless of department or office, has to realize that he has a grave responsibility, through his connection with a Catholic college, for being accurately informed about the position of the Church on historical and current issues.

Not the least result of faculty indoctrination, if it may be so called, will be an increase of humility through the submission of the intellect to truth and to authority. Human nature is inclined to partial and partisan views and teachers seem to be no less subject than the rest of mankind to a tendency toward selecting material that points up a preferential attitude. Frequent contact with an integrated body of truth is a healthful counter-agent to this temptation. It is a very good thing, too, for those who are constantly in a position of intellectual authority, to feel, themselves, the force of a firmly directive voice. Administrators, moreover, will find—we hope with constructive discomfiture—that the strong light of doctrine shows up flaws in policy and inconsistencies between profession and practice.

But how, practically, to get such a body of doctrine over to students? The strongest, simplest way, where the documents admit of classroom use, is to introduce them as part of the textual material of a course. For this, they must usually be available in English and the content should be logically suitable. It seems scarcely necessary to mention that any number would qualify for incorporation in political science, history, economics, sociology, journalism, and education courses, over and above those in philosophy and religion. Some language courses could employ appropriate documents for reading and translation: Spanish classes might read those on the Church in Spain and Mexico; French classes, those on France or any of the very large number published in French; German classes, those that have been printed in German, particularly the more recent ones; Latin, any of pertinent content, because practically all appear in Latin. Incidentally, an entire course on marriage and the home could be built on the encyclicals on marriage and Pius XII's sixty or more talks to newly married couples.

Documents of a content related to, but not an integral part of, a course can be used as references. Students in contemporary European history, for example, could have access in English to at least twelve out of nineteen encyclicals that would give first-hand and absolutely reliable information on conditions in Italy, Spain, France, Germany, Hungary, Poland, and Belgium, between 1882 and 1937.[15] Several others are available in French. There are, too, authoritative commentaries that would supply background and help with interpretation. The same thing would hold true for any number of courses, among them technique courses in English prose, which always have the problem of getting intrinsically worth-while material for students to work with.

Assignments involving reference work should include papal documents as a matter of course. This is the only way to get students into the habit of turning to them as an essential source of information and direction. The average student from the sophomore year up will have no more difficulty in reading these than he will anything else; in fact, if he is being brought up scholastically, he will have less. He will find respect for terms, accuracy of definition, orderly progress, logical relationships. In the writings of Pius XII, he will also meet an extraordinary concreteness of exposition and a striking facility in the rhythmic use of language.

A complete orientation course could be based on the pronouncements of Pius XII. He has talked directly to students and to other youth groups constantly since the beginning of his pontificate, and a great deal of what he has said to adults would also be within the reach of freshmen. Unfortunately, a good many of the best of these talks are untranslated, but need that be an insuperable obstacle to their use in a college?

The innumerable extra-class activities on an American campus open the way wide to getting students acquainted with Catholicity in thinking. International and interracial groups, the college Red Cross chapter, the youth membership of the Conference of Christians and Jews, the Confraternity of Christian Doctrine unit, clean literature pro-

---

[15] Sister M. Claudia, *Guide to the Encyclicals.*

moters, the National Student Association, the National Federation of Catholic College Students, the National Council of Catholic Women—all these and other organizations are earnest about what they are trying to do within student circles and through them. Again, how much more could be accomplished if students could visualize themselves as united with young people round the world in one great cause, no matter what their special interest or under what name they operate. This is the spirit of union and cooperation "in one mind" that the Holy Father wants to impress on the youth of all nations by the erection of the *Domus Pacis* at the center of Christendom.

Will students respond to the appeal and the discipline of truth as it comes to them through the basic synthesis of Thomism constantly and consistently applied to the problems of their own lives and their own social environment by the papal documents? Dare we say "no" without a more adequate educational program than most of us, probably any of us, can claim? Would it be presumptuous to say "yes" on the strength of one experiment?

A group of seventeen students selected from all departments—three sophomores, seven juniors, seven seniors—were invited to write a series of essays based on their personal investigation of an assigned subject connected with papal documents. All except three worked entirely with the documents of Pius XII. Their time was limited to approximately one month; they had to keep up their class attendance and meet regular course assignments; their "privilege" was to produce a paper that would meet rigid standards of accuracy and be reasonably creditable in style; their reward was to have their work printed.

Whatever may be said of the published result, the important question is: what did the project do for them? Did it contribute to their formation, in the broad sense of discipline: training which develops, strengthens, molds, and perfects?

According to the students' own account, the work itself was mentally taxing, physically fatiguing, time consuming, but thoroughly rewarding; it resulted, they felt, in a notable increase of power in research and accuracy of exposition. They were literally amazed at the scope of the documents and their authoritative treatment of secular as well as religious and moral topics. They were fascinated by the holiness, the devotedness (solicitude), the zeal, the energy, the application, the erudition, the literary facility, the personal charm of Pius XII. A single quotation will suffice to summarize their estimate of the research value of the project:

> From my research for the yearbook paper, I realized *many* things—that the Pope is one of the few, if not the only one, who has a true concept of the total world crisis; that his writings have concrete, positive solutions for every problem of our time; that we, as Catholics seem consistently to refer to every source for information on vital topics, except that of Christ's representative on earth today.
>
> The fact that the Church holds the only plan, at this point, for any future, I had previously so taken for granted that it meant nothing, but by only reading on my topic (youth), the fact struck home! We just aren't encyclical-conscious or Pope-conscious!

We who supervised the study also "realized many things"; of them, one is particularly important to this group. The Catholic college is in a preferred position for forming members—officer plus rank and file—of the only force that can hope to hold the citadel of Christian civilization against the attacks of a Marxist-headed social revolution. In spite of our knowledge of this fact, we educators have been notably neglectful of a complete treasury of training material incomparable for our purposes—the papal documents. Is not the very surprise of Catholic students at the all-embracing wisdom of the Holy See an acid-enough criticism to stimulate our colleges to concerted action in making papal pronouncements an integral part of every curriculum?

Discipline and Leadership Prestige

By REVEREND PAUL HANLY FURFEY

It must certainly be obvious to all of us that the quality of a college depends very directly on the quality of its faculty. The old saying that Mark Hopkins and a student on opposite ends of a log would have made a fine educational institution is worn rather threadbare, but it serves to remind one of an important fact. Buildings and grounds, equipment, record systems, and all the rest have their own importance; yet the fact remains that the fundamental educational process rests on the day-by-day contact between the student and teachers who are capable of winning and holding his respect, teachers with leadership prestige.

A good faculty does not simply appear at a college by chance. It must be the product of a definite policy. In the long run most colleges get the sort of faculty they deserve. If salaries are adequate, if working conditions are satisfactory, if opportunities for self-development exist and morale is high, then excellent teachers will compete for the opportunity of joining the faculty. If these things are absent, the college will find it hard to gather and hold even a mediocre staff. News circulates among teachers from one college to another and competent people gravitate to those institutions which have good reputations.

To attract good teachers the college must first of all pay adequate salaries. The administrator who is constantly hard pressed for funds may be tempted to remark that this is easier said than done. However, it is well to remember that teachers' salaries deserve a high priority in the expenditure of whatever funds exist. Justice requires that the teacher be paid a salary commensurate with his services. Moreover, an adequately paid faculty is an excellent investment from the purely financial standpoint. The college with a highly competent teaching staff will earn a fine reputation; it will grow and prosper. Large and ornate buildings may impress the casual visitor; but in the long run the worth of a college will be judged principally by the quality of its faculty.

Even in the case of religious who are vowed to poverty the college must be willing to spend money to get competent teachers. Money must be spent for unhurried graduate training. Then, after the religious has obtained the doctorate and has returned to teach at the college, money must be spent for his professional advancement. The religious, like the lay teacher, needs to buy books, subscribe to journals, pay dues in professional societies, attend meetings and conventions, and perhaps have a leave of absence for postdoctoral training or research. Spending money for these things does not violate the spirit of poverty. They have to do with the duty of the religious as a teacher, not with any personal and selfish satisfaction.

An adequate salary is an essential consideration for a teacher who must support himself, and possibly a family also; but it is by no means the only element which makes a teaching position attractive. There is, for example, the question of tenure. A college which expects to attract a strong faculty must be willing to give teachers permanent tenure after they have been at the institution long enough to prove themselves thoroughly. A lay teacher feels very insecure if he suspects that the religious community which runs the college is going to train one of its own members to replace him. The college should adopt a definite policy which should be clearly understood by administration and faculty alike, and this policy should cover salaries, promotions, tenure, and retirements, so that, if the teacher meets the standards of the college, he may look forward to a career there with security for himself and his family. If the college is not willing to offer this security to those who can qualify for it, faculty morale will suffer badly.

Working conditions are another point to be considered. The college should set definite standards for teaching loads and for the other services which the teachers are expected to perform; and these standards should be respected by both the faculty and the administration. A good teacher wants to grow in his subject. He wants time to read his professional literature, to carry on discussions with his colleagues, to rework his classes. If he is overloaded with an unreasonably heavy schedule, he cannot find time for these things, his work gradually becomes mere drudgery, and both he and his students lose interest.

The best teachers will be ambitious to do research, and they should be encouraged in every possible way. Some teachers merely toy with research and they do not deserve great consideration; but the man who has a strong drive toward original work is a very valuable person to have on the faculty and he deserves the best the college can give him. Association with a man who is doing first-class research can be an exciting intellectual experience for the students, and the presence of a few such men on the faculty can improve greatly the whole atmosphere of the college.

Good working conditions depend not only on the formal policies of a college, but also on a number of subtle factors which are not easy to define. A college can be a very pleasant place to work when the prevailing atmosphere is buoyant and cheerful and free from tension. It can be a very unpleasant place when interpersonal relations are stiff and formal, when suspicion is rife, and faculty politics are full of plots and counterplots. A college is indeed fortunate when its president and its executive officers have a genius for creating a friendly atmosphere, a genius which must rest on a solid basis of unfeigned Christian charity. It is not hard to get competent teachers to stay at such an institution. Certain recent studies in industrial sociology have shown that the efficiency of factory workers increases markedly when interpersonal relations are pleasant. College teachers, also, like to work in an atmosphere of friendliness and mutual trust. Under such conditions they will cheerfully overlook minor imperfections in the college organization.

A college which keeps to a high standard in its faculty personnel practices will have no difficulty in building up a corps of excellent teachers who will have prestige in the eyes of the students. Such a college will be able to pick and choose among prospective teachers, and an enormous amount of care should be exercised in the process of selection. In general, of course, there are two possibilities. The college may either hire teachers who are already trained or it may select promising candidates and send them away for graduate training. The latter alternative would apply particularly in the case of a religious community training prospective teachers from among its own members. In any case, very careful selection should be the rule.

In hiring teachers who are already trained, the great difficulty is to know the candidate sufficiently ahead of time. When a new faculty member is hired through a teachers' agency, the person who does the hiring must depend in making his decision on written documents, supplemented perhaps by a single interview. On the basis of such information it is hard to assess the more subtle personal qualities which often make the difference between an excellent and a mediocre teacher. It is much easier to make a wise decision if one knows the candidate well. When chairmen of departments regularly attend the meetings of their professional societies, they can often gain a great deal of valuable information. They get acquainted with the younger men in their field, including the graduate students. They follow the careers of these younger men and learn their reputation among their colleagues. When an opening occurs they have the facts which make it possible to pick the most promising candidates. Contacts of this sort are probably the most satisfactory basis for good teacher selection.

When a religious community selects one of its own members for graduate training, an equal amount of care is necessary. A good scholastic record is an obvious requirement. It is important also that the prospective trainee should have a real interest in his subject and a corresponding special aptitude. To teach English literature and to teach mathematics call for different types of ability. A teacher may do his best out of obedience to teach a subject which he hates, but he cannot communicate to his students an enthusiasm which he himself lacks. Sometimes it is good policy for a college to help a lay person financially so that he may complete his graduate studies and teach on the faculty. For example, a good teacher who has only an M.A. might be sent away to complete his work for the doctorate.

After a teacher has been selected and appointed as a member of the faculty, the problem of supervision arises. There can be no question about the fact that some sort of supervision is necessary. Young teachers can learn from older and more experienced teachers in supervisory positions. Ambitious beginners with the proper spirit will be happy to profit from the opportunity. The crucial point is the manner in which the supervision is given. Given ineptly, it can do more harm than good. The best supervisory direction can often take the form of apparently random remarks and bits of advice in the course of an informal conversation. A formal summons to the dean's office followed by a severe lecture may discourage a young teacher rather than help him.

Democratic discussions at faculty meetings can help a teacher to discover and remedy his faults. Some such topic as the examination and grading system is put on the agenda. Teachers discuss their difficulties and ways for overcoming them. Techniques are proposed and submitted to faculty criticism. The more successful and experienced teachers air their views and are listened to with respect. As the young teacher listens he begins to analyze his own work. He becomes conscious of his mistakes and learns to improve his methods. A dean who knows how to stimulate discussion of this sort will find the task of supervision easy. To a large extent, the faculty supervises itself, not through nagging and fault-finding but through the constant interchange of mutually helpful suggestions.

It is very important for a faculty to be able to work together as a team. The individual teacher must realize that he cannot educate a student single-handed. Education is a process which needs the coördinated effort of a faculty group. Education calls for teamwork. The teacher, therefore, should take pride in the success of the team of which he is a member. He should be anxious to do what he can to strengthen the faculty as a whole and should not be solely intent on his own individual success. The ability of a teacher to work smoothly with others is an important ability. This, also, should be taken into consideration when selecting teachers. A brilliant teacher is a questionable asset to the college if he is proud and oversensitive, full of selfish ambition, and unwilling to coöperate with others in a spirit of good teamwork.

A faculty quickly loses leadership prestige if it lacks a feeling of unity. Students are quick to realize that Dr. A does not like Dr. B and they learn to play off one against the other. They begin to take sides in faculty quarrels and they lose respect for the faculty as a whole. But when the members of the teaching staff are able to submerge their minor personal disagreements and to present a united front to the student body, their leadership is respected. Leadership prestige does not depend merely on the qualities of individual teachers; it depends on the smooth united efforts of the entire faculty. When all the members of the teaching staff seek in different ways to lead the students toward the same set of ideals, then their joint effect can be very powerful.

No one will follow a leader whom he does not respect. Therefore, it is very important that teachers should be persons of high character. Students have plenty of opportunity to observe and judge their teachers. They pass long hours together in the classroom, in the laboratory, in the various contacts of the general campus life. The teacher is on exhibition in all his varying moods. In the course of the school year a constant variety of situations arise, and the teacher's reaction to each one of these is observed. In the little world of the campus every teacher is a public figure; he is constantly in the public eye. All his personal characteristics are interesting subjects for campus gossip. Each teacher has his supporters and his opponents among the student body and his merits and demerits are debated pro and con. In the long run students are rather likely to form a fairly accurate estimate of the true character of every faculty member. Under this constant scrutiny a teacher must be a man of genuine worth to gain and hold leadership prestige in the campus world.

Students soon learn to distinguish various types among the members of the faculty. There is the teacher who courts popularity by setting low academic standards and making his class periods as painless as possible. He tells long and interesting stories which, however, have little relation to the matter at hand. He emphasizes nonessential aspects of his subject which are easy to lecture about. He skirts around the essentials which require hard intellectual effort if they are to be understood. His lectures are very easy to follow, but they are not very informative. He gives easy examinations and a high proportion of high grades. Naturally students flock to the courses of such a professor because it is only human to try to avoid work. A teacher of this type enjoys a superficial popularity, but he is not a real leader. Rather, he is being led. He is yielding to the desire of the poorer students to work as little as possible. It is really they, not he, who set the standards for his class.

Then there is the teacher who sets high standards, but who, by his poor teaching, makes it difficult for his students to reach those standards. His lectures are full of facts, but the facts are presented in such an uncoördinated fashion that the students cannot distinguish essentials and nonessentials. They cannot see the forest for the trees. He gives long reading assignments, but the students do not get much out of the books they read because they have not been properly trained to read their subject intelligently. Examination questions are worded so vaguely and ambiguously that the students are puzzled to know what the teacher is driving at. A great many students fail the course and the teacher prides himself on setting high academic standards, whereas the low grades which he gives are rather a reflection on his own lack of teaching ability. It is obvious enough that a teacher of this sort is not a real leader.

The good teacher sets a high standard, but he outlines his subject so clearly that any reasonably intelligent student who is willing to work hard can earn good grades. In his lectures this teacher picks out the essential principles and forcefully hammers them home. He makes sure that these principles are thoroughly understood. Once the students have grasped them, they find it is very easy to fill in the details. The teacher is constantly asking thought-provoking questions. Lazy students do not get much consideration in this teacher's classes; but those who are willing to work find them intensely stimulating. A teacher like this is a real leader. He, not the students, sets the standard. Yet, once he has set the standard, he is willing to go to any amount of trouble to help his students to come up to it. His classes are a challenge to genuine intellectual effort. Those students who accept the challenge are richly repaid.

Students soon find out whether the teacher has a genuine mastery of his subject or not. Of course it is easy enough to follow a textbook; but sooner or later classroom discussions will wander away from the text and then the teacher is really put to the test. The good teacher welcomes such discussions. He takes advantage of them to show the wider aspects of his subject. To him the textbook is merely an outline. His wide fund of knowledge permits him to bring in a wealth of illustrations. He shows the relations between the subject matter of his own course and the subject matter of other courses in the same field. He gives his students a sort of preview of more advanced courses and makes them eager to pursue their subject further. The good teacher is at ease in his subject. He is a leader because he personally embodies the ideal of sound and extensive scholarship.

If a teacher is unsure of himself, he cannot conceal that fact from his students very long. The insecure teacher will not tolerate any difference of opinion. Any objection suggested in class is a personal affront to him. Although distinguished authorities in his field may differ among themselves, he insists in his class that his own word is final and must not be questioned. The insecure teacher is afraid to say, "I don't know." It is a point of pride with him to answer every question, even though his answer may be transparently unsatisfactory. The insecure teacher is apt to overcompensate, by boasting, for his own feelings of inadequacy. He talks a great deal of the high standards of the university where he did his graduate work. In class he tells stories in which he himself appears as the hero. He tells his students about the compliments he has received. He takes a very critical attitude and constantly belittles the work of his colleagues in his field. He is afraid to admit the slightest gap in his own knowledge or the slightest defect in his own work. He imagines that he is impressing his students; but they know, better than he, that intellectual humility is a mark of greatness and they rightly interpret his lack of humility as a confession of insecurity. The insecure teacher cannot attain genuine leadership prestige.

A teacher gains increased respect in the eyes of the students if his work is recognized beyond the campus. If the teacher of public speaking is in demand as an after-dinner speaker, if the English teacher writes a successful novel, if the music teacher gives public recitals and is well received, students are apt to follow their classes with more respectful interest. It is impressive to find that one's teacher's work is cited in footnotes in serious books or to come across articles written by him in professional journals. A teacher who presents papers now and then before the meetings of learned societies or who is elected to office in them must enjoy a certain standing among his colleagues and students realize this. To be in demand as a lecturer or to be appointed on important boards and commissions is a compliment to a faculty member and the implications are not lost on the student body. The college should try to have on its faculty men with some standing in the learned world and in the general community because such men are likely to have qualities of leadership and to have a good effect on the students.

Faculty members must be able to hold the respect of their students not only as scientists and scholars, but also as persons of high Christian character. Anything mean or petty about them is disedifying to the students. Once there was a Latin teacher who knew that his supervisor was due to pay a visit to the class on a certain date. He therefore drilled the students on the same passage for a week. By that time even the dullest student was able to render an excellent translation, explain the syntax of every sentence, and answer questions about the general background of the passage. Of course, when the supervisor came he was very favorably impressed. Yet the students lost respect for their teacher. They knew that he had cheated to impress his supervisor. A friend of mine who was conducting an educational survey paid a surprise visit to a classroom a few days before a certain test was to be given and found the answers to the test written on the blackboard; the teacher was cheating and the students knew it. How can such teachers upbraid their students if the latter are found copying in examinations? A dishonest teacher, known as such to his students, is a cause of scandal in the literal sense of the term. Such teachers are not likely to be leaders; if they are, they lead their students in the wrong direction.

One of the most valuable virtues in a teacher is the sort of tact in dealing with students which is based on Christian charity. Harshness, rudeness, and lack of consideration are out of place in teacher-student relationships. It is indeed ethically justifiable to be discourteous to a student as a form of punishment, but there are better and more effective ways of punishing. Generally speaking, students will act toward the teacher as he acts toward them. If the teacher is uniformly kind and thoughtful, students will be pleasant and coöperative; but if the teacher is harsh, students may do their best to make life miserable for him.

The student who is doing poor scholastic work should be handled with great tact. He should never be publicly humiliated before his classmates. His poor record does not need to be dramatized; he is probably acutely aware of it already and very sensitive on the point. To scold such a student and ridicule him will simply serve to make him more discouraged. The teacher should take him aside and counsel him privately in a spirit of helpfulness. It may be possible to give the student some useful advice which will help him to improve his work. In some cases poor scholastic work may be merely a symptom of some deep-seated personal problem which demands more expert treatment than the ordinary teacher is able to give and in this case the importance of a professional counseling service in the college becomes evident. Yet, even if the teacher lacks the technical training to handle fundamental personal problems expertly, he can generally do at least some good by kindness and simple, commonsense advice.

Psychological studies on problem-solving show that the subject works very inefficiently when he is worried about his own inability and the possibility of failure, while anything that bolsters self-confidence immediately improves efficiency. The nagging and critical teacher who constantly scolds his students and ridicules their errors undermines their self-confidence and creates precisely the atmosphere in which good intellectual work is difficult. On the other hand, the teacher who cheerfully assumes that his students are capable, praising their successes and passing lightly over their failures, builds morale and gives his students confidence in themselves; with such encouragement they put forth their best efforts. Kindness toward students is an attractive Christian virtue, but it is also an excellent educational technique.

The simple, fundamental Christian virtues are the most important factors in the teacher's leadership prestige. Students cannot help respecting a teacher who is upright, honest, and kind. If the man is in addition an excellent scholar and a brilliant lecturer, then of course he is the ideal faculty member. But even the teacher who is only of average competence in his subject can do a great deal of good if he is outstanding in his personal character, conscientious in his work, and kind and helpful toward his students. Such a teacher is likely to have far more leadership prestige and to have a far better effect on the student body than his brilliant but sharp-tongued colleague who is proud, selfish, and unkind. Education is not concerned exclusively with the development of the mind, but with the harmonious development of the whole Christian personality.

It is appropriate to end this paper with the same thought with which it began. By and large, the quality of a college is the quality of its faculty. The most important single concern of the college administrator should be to build up the very best possible corps of teachers. They should be given adequate salaries, even if the budget must be pared to the limit elsewhere. Every effort should be made to provide good working conditions for faculty members with opportunities for constant development in their several fields. The selection of the best available teachers is a task of the utmost importance. Teachers who are highly competent in their fields of specialization, as well as outstanding in their character as Christians, will have great leadership prestige in the eyes of the students. With such a faculty, a college cannot but be outstandingly successful in its task of Catholic education.

Discipline, Integration, and Worry

By Marie A. Corrigan

Fifteen years ago a psychologist listed anxiety as the "most prominent mental characteristic of occidental civilization." Whether or not he had sufficient evidence of its actual incidence so to place it as a characteristic of our civilization is a question we need not decide here. We agree with his observation that modern man is beset by anxiety, even to the point of being puzzled and anxious about his own anxiety. Those of us who are entrusted with the education and upbringing of modern youth must recognize and try to cope with that condition.

Specifically, our purpose here is to give some thought to anxiety or worry as it is found in the college student. To do that it will be effective, perhaps, to consider first the general area of emotional adjustment, for fear—of which worry or anxiety is a phase—is only one of several emotions that leave their impact upon the intellectual, physical, and moral aspects of human activity. It is well to recognize that any or all of these emotions may affect the college student at one time or another.

Moore[1] defines human emotions as normally being "mental reactions to our appreciation of a situation." If our appreciation of a situation is appropriate, the emotional reaction will be normal; if our evaluation is distorted or exaggerated, the emotional reaction is likely to be inappropriate to the reality of the situation. Although theories of emotions are by no means in complete agreement, it seems that emotions vary not only in appropriateness but also in intensity and in their effect upon physical and mental processes. At one end of the scale we may place the mild emotional states which have a tonic effect on the physical and mental functions. Fear or anger of this kind often alerts the individual to caution and examination of the situation arousing the feeling. The pleasant emotions of joy,

---

[1] Thomas Verner Moore, *Personal Mental Hygiene* (New York: Grune and Stratton, 1944), p. 15.

love, and desire promote interest in and anticipation of the situation out of which they arise.

Further along the continuum, are strong emotions which seem to mobilize the mental and physical forces of the individual for action appropriate to the emotion. Even though appropriate, this re-organization may be violent. When the crisis is past, however, the body adjusts itself to resume normal activity. The effect of this occasional and brief onset of strong emotion is to concentrate the energies of the mind and body in one direction and to withdraw those energies from other directions. Some psychologists distinguish two effects of strong emotion: the active and the depressive effect. Although strong emotion usually tends to mobilize for action, grief, worry, or despair experienced by those who feel helpless in the face of the emotionally-toned situation may serve rather to depress activity. If the person in the grip of this emotion gains true insight into the situation evoking it, the feeling will not persist unduly long nor reach unendurable intensity. The crisis can be met adequately. Real insight, however, is dependent upon so many factors, among which are knowledge, personal endowments, training, and experience, that it is not attained by everyone in an emotional state; and one, therefore, expects to find abnormal emotion in many college students.

At the extreme of the continuum are emotional states of undue intensity or duration. In this state the individual may suffer from complete disorganization of physical and mental functions so that he becomes physically ill or loses touch with reality.

Fear and anxiety are emotions which may be found at any point on this scale of emotional intensity and duration. That fear or anxiety which promotes prudence in the face of a real or impending danger is normal and healthy. In the physical area it may prompt the student to protect his health and to avoid foolhardy risks to his own life or to that of another. In the social area it may encourage the development of social graces, regulate the choice of companions, stimulate social sensitivity and sharpen interest in social and political reform. In the spiritual realm it keeps one attentive to the state of his supernatural life and encourages development of his mental powers and special aptitudes.

This is the fear and anxiety which man feels when he has a fairly accurate and sensitive understanding of himself and the world in which he lives. It is this fear that the college does well to promote within its students by giving them an increasingly deeper and more mature understanding of themselves and the universe and society about them. This healthy feeling, however, is not as evident among college students as are abnormal fears. Few college students seem to fear the threat of secularism or economic injustices or are properly anxious about the sanctity of their classmates or other associates.

Healthy, normal fear and anxiety may become acute at times when a situation or condition demands concentration of mental or physical powers: a family financial crisis threatens the student's educational plans, a loved one is critically ill, a serious injustice has been visited upon one, an academic or social failure looms up. These acute emotional experiences will have no detrimental effect upon the student if they arise through real insight into the situation or condition stimulating them and if the pattern of emotional behavior evoked is appropriately mature.

Fear and anxiety, however, may also be found at the extreme of the scale. Here anxiety arises without a true appreciation of a situation. The danger is unreal, or if real, is greatly exaggerated. The emotion does not serve to stimulate or to marshal forces to overcome the danger, but prompts retreat and withdrawal not only from the danger itself but often from other activity. Various physical disorders may arise from a strong and persistent anxiety or fear. The person may also resort to certain psychological devices for avoiding the impending evil: regressive behavior, rationalization, development of symptoms of physical illness.

This brief and over-simplified outline of emotional reactions is intended to demonstrate that the task of the college is not to cushion the student against all feeling of fear but rather to assist him to gain the insight and to acquire the attitudes which will of themselves regulate emotional response to situations and conditions within and beyond college life. Over and above this also lies remedial work which is indicated for those students who have already established undesirable emotional behavior before entering upon their college life.

Those of us who are interested in the remedial or the developmental problems of emotional behavior in students must learn first of all that we cannot judge the reaction we observe in terms of the objective stimulus. If we do so judge, we will misinterpret much of what we observe and lose the opportunity to be helpful. The individual reacts to the situation in terms of its meaning and importance *to him*. What appears to us to be an unreasonable fear or resentment in another appears so because we see nothing which arouses in us fear or resentment. For us the situation furnishes no emotional stimulus. That does not demonstrate the absence of emotion-producing possibilities for another. A seasoned speaker, for example, may approach a speaking engagement without the slightest fear or anxiety —or with just enough to prompt him to give care to his preparation. That this is not solely a matter of practice or experience in speaking is indicated by the fact that one audience or assignment may make him relatively more fearful than does another.

One of the common causes of fear is the sense of impending loss of status or security. The infant who suddenly loses physical support experiences fear; the adult who has fallen from the state of grace is overwhelmed when he realizes his eternal insecurity and is afraid. Likewise, the speaker who approaches his audience has placed some value on that situation in its effect on his security or status. If he is sufficiently secure in relation to his audience, the speech is not a trial by which he may stand or fall. He has no fear. If, however, he doubts his status among them and if it is important to him to be found worthy of their approval, the speech takes on the nature of a trial and is accompanied by at least some degree of fear.

The particular pattern of behavior that emotion will take depends somewhat on the experience of the individual. In addition to the physiological reactions such as change in pulse rate or digestive and respiratory changes, there may be overt emotional behavior conditioned by past experience: the speaker may refuse the engagement; he may stutter or race through his talk at an abnormal rate; he may be unable to think while he is speaking; he may blush or grow pale or tremble; he may develop a severe headache or other ailment which will release him from the engagement without making it necessary for him to admit even to himself that he could not face the group and risk disapproval.

The desire for status and security in social units is commonly felt and is an entirely reasonable desire of a social being. Not only does man need others to minister to him but, as Maritain points out, man's inner urge to communicate knowledge and love requires others to whom these may be communicated. It is the part of education and maturity to make man discriminating in his choice of social units to which he seeks admission and in his knowledge of what is necessary in order to be secure in those units. Modern advertising, motion pictures, light literature, and conversation have set up false values in the requirements for social acceptance and status. This has the twofold effect of encouraging groups to accept or exclude others by these standards and of establishing within the individual desiring admission to the group false standards which he tries to meet and which he substitutes for more desirable and substantial social goals.

The college student comes into contact with several new social units: the faculty, his roommate, his own immediate classmates, the entire college population, and perhaps other social groups of which the college population is a part. It is reasonable and natural that he try to find status and security within several of these units. The prospect and process of so doing is likely to evoke some fear and anxiety. The nature and extent of this emotional reaction to the new social situations will depend upon several factors: the status the individual desires to attain; the standards he judges, rightly or wrongly, that he must meet; the experience he has already had in finding social acceptance; the attitude of each group toward him.

Not only is the college situation itself likely to arouse varying degrees of fear within students, but each student also brings with him his own peculiar and normal sources of anxiety, such as family affairs, plans for the future, economic and ethical problems, and innumerable other possibilities. Add to these anxieties, which have some reasonable cause, the multitude of fears for which students cannot account or which, if they could, would be found to be groundless, and we have reason to agree that anxiety and fear are registered on every college campus.

As we have said before, the student has already set many patterns of emotional reaction and behavior long before he has reached the college. These, however, will undergo some change, and it is in part the responsibility of the college to promote desirable alteration of emotional patterns.

That responsibility, it seems to me, grows out of the fact that the college is recognized as one means whereby a person may grow in his ability to perform various human acts. The human act depends upon the reflection of the intellect, the activity of the will, and the freedom of the will to exercise choice. All educational institutions recognize their obligation to make available to the student information and principles upon which the intellect may reflect. Some institutions also recognize an obligation in the development of the will. Few, however, take into account the factors which affect the freedom of the will. We are concerned here with only one of these factors, that of emotion. Although few educators have crystallized their thinking on their responsibility in the emotional area of the student's life, it would seem that once having noted the impact that emotions have on the use of the intellect and the will, they would find it impossible to ignore this factor in the education of a student.

Father O'Brien,[2] drawing from the writings of St. Thomas, sums up the effect of emotion in this way: "Passion can impede the perfection of a human act by impairing directly the function of advertance, or by indirectly impairing the consent of the will, or by restricting the exercise of liberty."

He goes on to explain the manner in which emotion may impair the reflection of the intellect and the operation of the will:

> Passion may produce inadvertence (1) by preventing the agent from actually adverting to what he knows habitually; (2) by distracting the agent from considering in the particular what he knows in the universal; (3) by producing through its concomitant bodily change an impediment to the actual use of reason which must operate in a physically disturbed organism.

---

[2] Vergil Patrick O'Brien, *The Measure of Responsibility in Persons Influenced by Emotion* (Washington D.C.: Catholic University of America Press, 1948), p. 2.

Passion may indirectly impair the perfection of the consent of the will by directly disturbing the function of the intellect which must precede the will act.

Passion may restrict the liberty of the agent if the movement of the sensitive appetite is so powerful as to absorb totally the attention of the agent, so that he cannot consider anything else and sees no other course of action save to follow the dictate of passion.

Fear and anxiety may not affect the intellect and the will as strongly as do their other emotions, particularly anger; nevertheless, these emotions may serve, in one form, to stimulate human effort and, in more intense manifestations, to interfere seriously with the effective operation of the intellect and the freedom of the will.

Granted that the college student is subject to anxiety in many forms and from many stimuli and granted that the college must help the student reach emotional maturity in this as well as in other areas, a practical question arises: what can be done to assist the student? There is no single formula or method. The type of help offered will depend upon the needs of the individual student and upon the training, skill, and position of the educator. Some aid may be given to groups but some must be offered to the student as an individual apart from the group. Some will be part and parcel of any good college program, but some may consist of additional and special services.

Space will not permit an exhaustive discussion of means whereby students may be aided to gain emotional maturity; it may be helpful, however, to provide a few examples of means which can be employed.

First, all those who deal with the student in administrative, teaching, or other capacities ought to recognize the nature and power of emotions, so that the college environment itself may further emotional maturity, or at least not become an obstacle in the attainment of that goal. It is common for teachers in elementary and secondary education to be required to study principles of mental hygiene for the effect this study has both on their own mental health and on that of their students. It might be well for college teachers to follow their lead by at least reading a good treatment of the subject.

Out of this appreciation of emotional factors may come more desirable classroom and administrative procedures together with a readiness to adjust temporarily routine or work when a student is in an emotional crisis. If the crisis does not pass reasonably soon or if the emotional behavior is otherwise questionable, those working with the student ought to recognize this condition and make an appropriate referral for help.

Second, strong emotion ought not be evoked for disciplinary purposes. If our brief examination of the nature of emotions has been at all useful, it can readily be seen that normally strong emotion is a transient condition. Fear, the emotion we are considering here, directs the mental and physical resources in one direction in order to protect the individual or his interests. When the protective measure has been taken or the danger passes, these resources resume their normal roles. If fear persists for a long time or with great intensity, normality is not regained; and the physical and mental health of the person is thereby endangered.

The use of strong fear as a disciplinary measure has practical limitations if evoked as an occasional and transient emotion, for discipline and motivation cannot be occasional matters. If, on the other hand, strong fear is cultivated as a constant threat, the student's physical and mental powers may operate at an inefficient level. Sarcasm in the classroom, unpredictable enforcement of regulations, severe threats of failure for infringement of rules are common and often effective means of arousing strong fear and anxiety in the student. In some cases, these evoke not only fear but also despair, a feeling of helplessness in the face of the circumstances. In a student new to the institution, the rejection implied in sarcasm and severe threats also serves to indicate that he is not acceptable in this particular social unit: the classroom, the faculty, or administration. That, in turn, may set up a new fear or anxiety if acceptance by the unit is important to him.

Many who use strong fear as disciplinary means are sincere in their desire to have a salutary effect upon the minds and wills of those with whom they are working. Their own personal temperamental difficulties or a misunderstanding of emotional reactions leads them to choose unsuitable means. The motivational value of emotions is by no means denied; this value, however, is greatest when the emotion arises out of insight into a situation and is tempered by sound attitudes.

That suggests a third means by which the college may promote emotional maturity; namely, by developing attitudes which will stimulate appropriate emotional responses to situations or conditions. Allport,[3] in defining attitude, speaks of its "directive or dynamic influence upon the individual's response to all objects and situations with which it is related." Part of this response is emotional.

The student does not arrive free from intellectual habits, or attitudes, so the task of the college here is twofold: to correct undesirable attitudes and to form new intellectual habits. The first way the educator does this is through the teaching of facts and principles, for it is upon these that attitudes ought to be founded. Since attitudes may begin with life itself, however, it is obvious that many of them may be formed not on truth but on half-truths, incomplete information, or be adopted from others who had formed them out of the fabric of their own scanty knowledge.

With this condition the college cannot be satisfied, for the mature, well-balanced person has a store of attitudes which, when examined in the light of reality, are valid. The first contribution of the college, then, in this area is to teach a body of information and principles by which old attitudes may be revised or new ones formed.

We have to mention only a few subjects upon which emotionalized attitudes are held to see the possibilities: politics, the role of government, marriage, the race question, criteria of economic success. Upon each of these, as upon a hundred other subjects, many persons have strong attitudes which, while they may not even be consciously held, influence decisions.

The college teacher, however, is faced with another problem when he wishes to teach principles or facts which are contrary to those upon which the individual has built his attitudes. This arises from the fact that one tends to accept more readily those new ideas that somehow fit into the pattern of ideas already set up. Even when the new attitude is apparently accepted, the old attitude may prevail in its influence on decisions and emotional reactions. This has

---

[3] G. W. Allport, "Attitudes" in *Handbook of Social Psychology.* Carl Murchison, ed. (Worcester, Mass.: Clark University Press, 1935), p. 810.

been treated by many, among whom are Newman with his distinction between notional and real assent and Schanck[4] with his conclusion that people may hold attitudes as members of institutions which are inconsistent with or quite different from their private or personal attitudes.

Three of the most common ways of changing a concept already established are: by repeated experiences which demonstrate the validity of a new concept; a single sharp, dramatic or perhaps traumatic experience which makes a radical change in an old concept; and a permissive psychological climate in which a concept may be examined objectively without need for defense. So the college teacher in developing new attitudes must not only present the facts and principles needed to establish the desired attitude, but he must also present these in such manner that they will be assimilated by the student into the context of his own thinking. This may be done by providing repeated experiences which will emphasize the new concept, or it may be done by setting up the favorable climate mentioned above.

Closely allied to attitudes are the values held by a person. Wells[5] equates adjustment with "the attainment of what is valued" and maladjustment with "the failure to attain it." The attitudes and values held by an individual are highly important in the emotional life. They give meaning to the experiences he has and in that way prepare the way for the emotional response to be evoked by the experience. They also direct his desires, thereby indicating the bases upon which his adjustment shall rest. It is the saintly person who has the greatest opportunity for being essentially well-balanced. His appreciation of reality embraces the supernatural; his values are properly ordered, and his faith and hope make him confident of attaining that which he values.

If the college had no other reason for inculcating desirable attitudes and values than that of developing emotional maturity, the desirability of this educational outcome

---

[4] R. L. Schanck, "A Study of a Community and Its Groups and Institutions Conceived of as Behaviors of Individuals," *Psychological Monographs*, XLIII, No. 2 (Princeton: Psychological Review Co., 1932), 133.

[5] F. S. Wells, "Social Maladjustments: Adoptive Regression" in *Handbook of Social Psychology*. Carl Murchison, ed. (Worcester, Mass.: Clark University Press, 1935), p. 810.

would be sufficient to warrant our making every effort to discover and to use effective means of doing so.

The fourth contribution of the college lies in helping the student to develop mature emotional behavior. So far we have been concerned with emotional stimulus and reaction. Here we bring into focus the manner in which the person acts while in an emotional state. Again we look toward maturity as an ideal. In its report a committee of the American Council on Education[6], assigned to study "emotions and the educative process," summarizes three criteria of mature emotional behavior:

> *A genetic criterion* of mature behavior would demand the achievement of patterns of affective behavior that are effective in resolving physiological tensions and disequilibria and that result in a strong hedonic tone of pleasure in carrying out of fully integrated behavior.
>
> *A social or cultural criterion* of mature behavior would demand the achievement of patterns of affective behavior such as are common and accepted within the population of a given area, and the avoidance of patterns of affective behavior which run counter to the mores or which arouse tension and antagonistic action in a considerable number of other persons.
>
> *An ethical criterion* of mature behavior would demand the achievement of patterns of affective behavior that conform to certain basic value principles which are accepted by a given individual or population, and the avoidance of patterns of affective behavior that are contrary to these value principles in their effect upon oneself or upon others.

The committee points out the impossibility of using any one of these criteria by itself: the physiological criterion in many cases would run counter to the social and cultural criteria. The social criterion is not consistent within itself inasmuch as society narrows or widens the range of behavior it accepts as mature with various kinds of persons and under various conditions. For instance, it condones in the college student that which it frowns upon in the adult, accepts in the man with prestige that which it does not permit to the common man. Furthermore, society would quickly stagnate were there no social rebels to maintain progress.

---

[6] American Council on Education. *Emotion and the Educative Process*, Daniel A. Prescott, Chairman (Washington: American Council on Education, 1938), pp. 98-101.

The Committee found itself "almost . . . at an impasse" when it had to admit that it could not advance unchallenged the ethical criterion because "many persons do not admit that absolute ethical values exist." The Catholic college finds itself at no such impasse and must help its students develop mature emotional behavior which, first of all, conforms to ethical standards and then to whatever social and genetic criteria are not in conflict with the ethical standards.

Fear and anxiety usually do not stand as isolated emotions but often are accompanied by anger, resentment, or even hatred. There are well-defined principles of charity and justice whereby the normal person who is subject to these emotions may be expected to act. In addition, there are certain social and genetic criteria that ought to regulate behavior arising out of an emotional experience. The conscious development of standards of mature emotional behavior is highly important today when the individual is bombarded by emotional stimuli and when choices of an emotional nature are so often governed solely by the physiological criterion, based on the release of physical tension.

The fifth contribution of the college may be to assist the student to examine his own pattern of emotional behavior and his emotionalized attitudes so that he may consciously set out to modify these if necessary. For the most part this is a specialized task to be undertaken by a spiritual director, a trained counselor, or a psychiatrist, or even a combination of these persons, as the individual problem seems to indicate. Occasionally, however, the teacher, by enabling the student to discuss fully in a group or alone his ideas and concepts, may assist him to examine these objectively.

The opportunity to examine one's concepts and attitudes is important not only in its effect upon the emotional life of the student but also upon his intellectual activities. Reasoning is often based upon attitudes and principles of which the person is unaware. In studying this problem some time ago, Miriam Dunn found that the major premise was subconscious in twenty-five percent of the reasoning she analyzed. Moore[7] points out that these principles which lie

---

[7] *Op. cit.*, p. 102.

below the level of focal consciousness may give rise to both reasoning and conduct which are pathological because
  (1) the mind harbors a number of false principles;
  (2) the principles are fixed in the mind because of their emotional resonance and the fact that they are essential to the system of desires that has been woven into the very fabric of mental life; and
  (3) the principles are suppressed into the unconscious because, if viewed by focal consciousness, they would reveal the unworthiness of one's conduct.

We are concerned here with the emotional significance of attitudes and concepts which one has never subjected to adult, objective examination. Concepts, attitudes, and principles which give rise to anxiety and fear are not uncommon and may be basic to the thinking that students do in relation to ethical and moral matters, vocational choices, family life, and filial obligations. To bring these out for examination may be easy or difficult, depending upon the individual's ability to formulate them into terms he himself understands and accepts. In many cases a spiritual director or a counselor can provide the permissive, psychological atmosphere in which the individual may examine his concepts and attitudes without becoming defensive about them. In other cases, it may be advisable that a psychiatrist assist the person to discover the origin of concepts and attitudes by reconstructing the experience or conditions under which they were formed.

A sixth way in which the college student can be assisted is in the development of competencies which will lessen the possibility of frustration, deep anxiety, and despair. The competencies needed are those which will give him entrance into and status within social units which are or ought to be important to him.

Often the student entering college lacks even the elementary social graces that put him at ease in the new groups with which he mingles: ease of manner, skill at dancing or bridge, care in his appearance, conversational facility. The college may provide opportunities for the incoming student to learn some of these quickly and easily and may at the same time undertake to highlight certain other qualities or abilities within these students so that their acceptance will not depend upon the skills which they lack. This is a service which older students or student leaders in the college may very well undertake, not only because of their strategic position in the institution but also because of the experience it gives them in searching out and appreciating commendable qualities within others.

Some institutions endeavor to restrict the expenditures made for clothes and luxuries so that class distinctions based on wealth may be eliminated. This appears to be an artificial approach to the problem, and at best is a temporary means of lessening the barriers to social acceptance. The positive emphasis is to be preferred.

More important than the development of competence which will enable the student to gain entrance into the smaller social units mentioned is the cultivation of a consciousness of the significant role to be played by the individual in the larger or more permanent units that will make up his life. Modern man is often frustrated by a deep sense of his unimportance and insignificance in life. There are few natural frontiers to be conquered by the ordinary man, few occupations normally clamoring for workers, little to challenge the average person in his daily life. And yet this picture of the insignificance of man is superficial: his importance in the Divine Plan, his role in the Mystical Body, his opportunities for Catholic Action are tremendous. This significance, however, is not self-evident; but the Catholic college ought to turn out graduates in whom a true sense of destiny and significance is awakened and in whom this feeling and knowledge will deepen throughout life. This true recognition of one's role in life leaves man truly humble but also protects him from the frustration of a purposeless existence. On such frustration is built much of the anxiety and fear of man.

Finally, the college may aid the student to gain maturity in regulating his fears and anxieties by providing each student enough training and experience of an aesthetic and cultural nature to give him a means of releasing tension when it occurs from the ordinary stimuli he will encounter. The American Council on Education Committee on Emotions and the Educative Process also emphasizes the value of aesthetic training and experience as a means of identifying oneself with a cultural group. This particular outcome of such experience gives the individual one more means of finding a place in a social unit which will be congenial to him.

With this suggestion we conclude our discussion of a few of the means whereby the college may assist the student to gain emotional maturity. Although we have confined our remarks largely to fear and anxiety as it appears in the college student, much of what has been said may be applied to other emotions which man experiences. In all of these, the college ought to aid the student to gain the emotional maturity which is promoted by insight into particular situations and conditions and by an appreciation of their true significance in one's life. This may be accomplished in part by the general aims and activities of the institution and in part by specialized services offered by those trained to work with emotions.

Discipline, Integration, and the Conditions of Leisure*

By John Julian Ryan

The reason why we are considering here today in the same paper the topics of discipline, integration and the conditions of leisure is that a sense of leisure, properly understood, is at once the ideal state of mind for mastering a liberal art and for achieving the all-round integration proper to a liberal artist; therefore it is one of the principal goals to be aimed at in the discipline of a Catholic college. I shall begin, then, by analyzing this ideal state of mind; proceed to an analysis of the teaching methods, administrative policies, and general conditions that would best foster it; and, finally, offer some concrete suggestions as to how we might go about improving our educational techniques in the light of these two analyses.

But first, before plunging into particular questions, may I indicate what I mean by a sense of leisure in education? Throughout this paper I shall use the term to mean that state of peaceful inner harmony enjoyed by a student who is advancing happily, with no avoidable distraction or strain, in the steady and liberal acquisition of the basic forms of skill known as the liberal arts. I shall try, that is, to give the term the sense which it had in the original Greek word from which we get the word *school*.

Now, what are the components of this ideal state of mind —this ideal attitude and mood—of the student in setting forth to master a liberal art?

First of all, he should be, as I think we shall all admit, in a state of enthusiasm; and this, not simply because we forget easily what bores us (or we remember it with a paralyzing distaste—for which reason, incidentally, I have often thought how sensible it would be for some teachers of the classics to use as texts the works of heretics) but also because enthusiasm is, in the best sense, leisurely and efficient. The profoundly enthusiastic student is one who is

---

* See Author's note following this paper.

inspired by an apostolic love, charity, for those whom he is to serve, God and his fellow-men; by a love of the object he has to attain in serving them; of the objectives it implies; of the knowledge these require; of the technique, the good form, to be exercised in attaining these objectives; of his co-workers, of his masters and the master artists and scientists of the past; of his training school and all its customs and instrumentalities. Such various affections as these promote leisure directly since they relax—all love is expansive and relaxing—and they all inspire the student to search deeply, hence with a liberal disinterestedness, into the fundamentals of the art being studied. They focus his attention undistractedly on what he is doing, generating the highest form of concentration, that of zeal. Then, too, because of the fact that "almost anyone can learn anything he really wants to learn," the enthusiasm born of these many affections shortens the learning time of any one art, and thus increases the time available for them all.

As a source of enthusiasm there must be, I should say, a profound delight in achieving and achievements—a true sense of the "fun," if you will, of work and study, not essentially different from that experienced in the playing of strenuous games. Naturally, nothing worth while is done without some drudgery; and every student should expect to endure it, both in mastering the art now and in practising it in the future. But true leisure is the result of a delight which carries one through drudgery without strain or boredom.

Negatively, the student must be at least free of dislike of his object and his means and methods. Certainly, he must be free of the fears that might paralyze him; of any vague feeling that what he is setting out to do is silly and "unrealistic"; that the whole process of education is pretty artificial, "academic," inhuman and unnatural; that he probably has not the talent, the assistance, the means, necessary for doing the thing right; hence, that he will simply fail—and not only fail but have a nervous and tense time in so doing.

As I have said elsewhere, the two greatest enemies of skill are timidity and tension, because they ruin the necessary leisure of the student. And the student who falls prey to these enemies will be in danger not merely of failing once, but of setting up a habit of failure. Having failed the first time because he was paralyzed by timidity and tension, he is liable even more surely to fail the second, since the first failure only makes him more fearful of the second and so more tense than at the first. The elimination, as far as possible, of the fear of failure in students who honestly wish to make the effort to become educated is, therefore, of paramount importance in the assurance of a true sense of leisure.

Specifically, then, the student should not be plagued by the feeling that he has not the time in which to go properly through the full stages of learning; that is, through the stages of familiarization, maturation, practice, appreciation, integration, and adjustment. He should not be given the worrisome sense of skipping any of these stages or of skipping through all of them. Rather, he should be given the joy of coming to know a subject exactly as an expert comes to know it and as he himself comes to know a friend—with a minimum of learning by rote and a maximum of absorption. Nor must he be made to feel discontent with the fact that it takes some things longer to "sink in" than it takes others (as if there were no such thing as assimilation or maturation, in the sense, especially, of Wm. James' "summer skating"). Again, he must feel free to carry out a full investigation or to work out a difficult problem or to practice whatever he needs to practice in acquiring a method, especially of his own, as he needs to practice it—all without strain or hurry or impatience. Nor should he be cheated of the chance to enjoy the rightness of whatever he is able to do—stepping off quietly to study it and see that it is good—as God "stepped off," as it were, and saw that the world was good. Further, he must have the freedom to meditate upon the significance of everything he does, never moving until he sees *why*, never feeling he is taking "time out" when he stops to appreciate all the aspects of what he learns—the beauty as well as the truth and goodness of it. And he must feel that it is simply part of the whole learning process to correlate and integrate all his various kinds of knowledge and skill. Then, he must feel that there is always some regular time for stopping and taking stock and readjusting his aims and plans accordingly—with the technical possibility of taking counsel, psychiatric as well as spiritual and ascetic, of re-educating himself without having to feel that he is getting hopelessly "behind in his work." Finally, he should feel free at all times to indulge in the equivalent of mathematical recreations—to browse or to take a purely voluntary course, if only to find out where his "natural" interests and talents lie.

Such being the attitude or state of mind which it is desirable for the student to maintain (in the truly "scholarly" state of mind), the next question is, obviously, what would be the *ideal* methods or means for aiding him to maintain it? With these sketched out, we can perhaps make out some practical ways of modifying our present methods accordingly.

What would, then, ideally assure the sense of leisure thus far described: what methods of teaching and training; what selections of teachers; what curriculum and activities; what methods of marking; what equipment and architecture?

Well, it would seem to be fairly obvious that the two main determinants of the answers to these questions are freedom from hurry and freedom from worry. That college would be ideal as a place of leisure in which the teachers would have the time to deal with each student personally, in private or semi-private tutoring, like that which produced the medieval university and is still carried on at Oxford. The work could then be assigned in accordance with the needs of the student; with his need to be made enthusiastic, to spend this or that amount of time on each of the processes described above (familiarization with the field, maturation, practice, meditation and appreciation, integration, adjustment to this or that failure). Because a tutor could keep a close watch over his students, he would be able to bring them along quietly and steadily, each at his own pace. The teacher himself would also have to be granted the prerequisites of leisure: using mainly one room or office and not having to rush about from one room (or, as often, one building) to another. He would not so much be "free to publish" as free to teach; free of economic worries, though not free to be luxurious; he should be able, because of his moderate teaching load, to lead a full, human life easily and unhurriedly; able, in short, to show his students by example what normally-paced living looks like.

The curriculum would be limited to basic courses with little or no specialization permitted—the theory being that any intense specialization may threaten the leisure required for full training in all the arts and may prevent a student from spending his time in calmly becoming a man before becoming this or that special kind of man. Again, it is obvious that since the fear of not covering the ground is one of the fears most destructive of true leisure, ideally the curriculum itself would be made as simple as possible; the subjects covered in each course would be those which a prospective artist-in-living, not a prospective "specialist in the field," would need; and the emphasis would be on training the student in the method which would enable him to proceed on his own after graduation, the assumption being that he would naturally continue to lead an intellectual life after leaving college. So, too, because ease in marking means frequent tests, preparation for which often destroys any possibility of going through in an unhurried or peaceful way the stages of learning described above, such tests would be reduced to a minimum and the grading of them would be done in words, not in numerals. Further, outside activities that consume time would be limited in accordance with the schedule of each student, none being permitted which might make him into a "hustler." Then, too, only the ability that is finally attained would be judged; early marks should not be averaged with late; the student would be encouraged to take his time and not worry if at first he found the going rough. As for equipment and buildings, everything would be done to assure the student of an atmosphere of Christian peace and of what might be called human surroundings. These should have about them nothing of the factory, nothing of mass production, nothing of routine, nothing of the prison-like, the "institutional," the puritanical, the stiff, the prim, the proper, the cold, the ugly, the "respectable," or the second-rate. And here I may be permitted to quote Stephen Leacock's brilliant humorous essay, "Oxford as I see it."

> The real thing for the student is the life and environment that surrounds him. All that he really learns, he learns in a sense by the active operation of his own in-

tellect and not as the passive recipient of lectures. And, for this active operation, what he really needs most is the continued and intimate contact with his fellows. Students must live together and eat together, talk and smoke together. Experience shows that that is how their minds really grow. And they must live together in a rational and comfortable way. They must eat in a big dining-room or hall, with oak beams across the ceiling, and the stained glass in the windows, and with a shield or a tablet here or there upon the wall, to remind them between times of the men who went before them and left a name worthy of the memory of the college. If a student is to get from his college what it ought to give him, a college dormitory with the life in common that it brings, is his absolute right. A university that fails to give it to him is cheating him.

If I were founding a university—and I say it with all the seriousness of which I am capable—I would found first a smoking room; then when I had a little more money in hand, I would found a dormitory; then after that, or more probably with it, a decent reading-room and a library. After that, if I still had money over that I couldn't use, I would hire a professor and get some text-books.

Now, I do not, of course, expect that you will all hasten back, as soon as this Workshop is over, to your respective colleges and suggest to the authorities that they close all the buildings except one and start afresh with this as a smoking-room. But perhaps I can make a few suggestions about what we need to do which we also may be able to do, if we are to make our institutions into places of true leisure.

The first thing which we should and can do here is, I think, learn to look upon the process through which we are putting the student as more of an apprenticeship than a studentship, and assure him as a consequence of the conditions of leisure that go with an apprenticeship. We must learn to see our work as putting the student through a complex set of processes (of familiarization, etc.), of slow stages of development and increase in skill. Furthermore, we must see that no matter how much more important any one of these processes may be than another, each of them is essential. Invention is no less necessary to a full training than is investigation, and integration is as essential as either. We should see that what are frequently thought of as digressions by the teacher intent on "covering the ground"—I am not here referring to his divagations into hobbies, but rather to those moments in which he dares to "bootleg wisdom" instead of handing out information—we should realize that such apparent digressions are in fact the most essential parts of the training. Moreover, we should learn to think in terms of the flexible scheduling required for permitting, as far as possible, each student to spend the amount of time on each process that he, and perhaps no one else in the class, needs to spend on it. In short, the first step we must learn to take here is that of convincing ourselves that the leisure required for an apprenticeship is a *sine qua non*, not a luxury—something so essential that without it we are simply not educating in the liberal arts at all but are only helping the student to stock his mind rather hurriedly with various forms of not very well assimilated scientific information.

Next, I should like to suggest that we ourselves take the time—be leisurely enough in our approach—to generate, by such methods as those suggested in more than one talk in this and other workshops, an intense, in fact a life-long enthusiasm for our subject. It is in the interests of leisure as well as of other requirements that we do so; for two reasons: one is, as I have said before, that the enthusiastic student learns more quickly than the unenthusiastic and therefore assures himself more time for the other studies as well as for the given one; the other is that if a student is inspired with a life-long enthusiasm for a study, he can be trusted, as he should be, to go on for himself in the pursuit of it, so that he will not need to have it presented to him in full detail in college. The student who is given an intense love of the Mass, for example, can certainly continue to grow daily in the art of worship it requires and in which it trains him. The student who is once given a Platonic love of philosophic discussion—of dialectics—will continue to philosophize more and more skillfully for the rest of his days, especially if he has been given expert guidance in the conduct of "bull-sessions." So, for the student who has been given a deep love of history, or economics, or politics, or the rest. He can be entrusted to explore assiduously the implications of the Papal Encyclicals on these subjects, in a spirit of fruitful leisure, once he has acquired a thorough basic, and it need not be more than a thorough basic, familiarity with them.

We must therefore resolve to take every precaution we can to assure our students of these two things: the enthusiasm and the fundamental habits that together give them what is called the principle of growth in their studies. This twofold requirement means particularly that we must not be afraid at any time in the course, but especially at the beginning of it, to "waste time" in getting down to the very deepest fundamentals and in assuring the very highest necessary skill in dealing with these. I say, especially at the beginning of a course, for obviously unless the student gets a clear firm grasp of the object, the objectives, the necessary requirements, the basic technical principles of an art, as well as of the realm of discourse of the science that it implies (the formal object, the processes, the factors of it, and the basic norms, definitions, postulates, axioms, methods of experimentation, verification, and formulation it uses) so that he has a rational understanding of the whole intent and pattern of a course—unless he gets these things, he will become a young artist only with great difficulty and much back-tracking, finding out almost by accident "what it is all about." And he cannot be expected to delve into fundamentals as deeply as all this implies unless he is made enthusiastic about his subject and unless he is given the opportunity to view and review fundamentals, to practice basic techniques again and again—at periods when he is at least undistracted. I stress this last requirement of the need for not being distracted, since it is one that is almost always ignored today. The very time when a student is most distracted—either as a newcomer finding his way about the campus, making friends, absorbing the spirit of the place, and so on, or as an upper-classman making the transition from vacation to school once again, with a hundred and one adjustments not unlike those of a newcomer—this is the very time during which the introductory lectures on the basic principles of a subject are given or the first chapters, philosophically the most important chapters in the book, are assigned for what amounts to cursory reading. Could any "method" for assuring a dampening of the student's enthusiasm or for failing to equip him properly for his venture be more effective than this? Whatever we can do to change this custom, whether it be simply to spend the first three or four weeks in inspiring the student with a desire to master a subject or in showing him how it fits into his whole course of training, whatever we do here will be, I believe, of almost incalculable value as a source of leisure, especially if we are ourselves truly leisurely in doing it.

Next, and this is something that is closely related to the previous suggestion, we should try not to hurry the students along as if they were capable of inorganic growth, like a building that grows bigger with each stone. It is absurd to suppose that every doctrine can be mastered in exactly the same time; that is, at the moment it has to be mastered if a student is to cover a whole subject, the schedule being determined by the articulation of the textbook, not by the learning habits of the student. And it is still more absurd to suppose that the mastery of an act of skill requiring the application of that doctrine, that an artistic "habit" can be assured with clockwork (or shall we say "lock-step") regularity. At the very first moment when a student is made to feel that he is queer if he cannot conform, certainly at the moment when he begins to feel the necessity for "hustling" if he is to "keep up"—at that moment he begins to lose the very leisure that might have been his only salvation.

Above all, we must never cause a student to worry or to lose enthusiasm for the training we provide as a result of feeling that, after all, the whole business is something at which he would not want to succeed. We must do all that we can to show him that it is not the "eager beaver," the model gentleman, the boy orator, or the quiz-kid, or their equivalents among young women, that we are trying to turn out; that we think as little of mere knowledge-machines as does any normal student; that we are interested in turning out whole men, well trained to be the all around priest-prophet-maker-rulers they were meant to be. If we are to keep the enthusiasm for learning in the normal student and rid him of the dislike of an unnatural training and the self-distrust born of not being able to conform to it, we must have the courage, I think, to award honors *never* to those students who have *only* exceptionally good set of marks, but *only* to those whom the faculty judges to be well-rounded personalities, capable of continuing to become more and more skillful and profound liberal artists.

Once a student saw that it was by his whole personality that he was being judged and that he was being given normal opportunities to grow before being so judged, he would be freed of one of the worst enemies of leisure, the anxiety caused by not being able to gain the highest grades.

Naturally, there should be no sense of being policed or regimented. College students are not so far from their childhood as not to relish playing "cops and robbers" with themselves as robbers. As we all know, the amount of time, to say nothing of the ingenuity, that is wasted in this kind of game, in not doing assignments, is far greater than that which would be required for doing them. Moreover, the suspicion that learning must be unnatural, that it must be something to be acquired only under strict compulsion and artificial rewards, inevitably robs a student of the enthusiasm of true leisure.

And here we have another set of reasons for our taking our time and, in a leisurely way, generating enthusiasm. For there is a direct relationship between the degree of enthusiasm of the student and the amount of policing he needs—the more of the one, the less of the other—so that we may well learn to ask ourselves just how economical in the long run it really is to rush into a subject, rather than to spend time in enabling the student to acquire a taste for it and to come to grips with it naturally and easily.

But if the student is not to be required to live up to an absurdly mechanical schedule of homework, if he is not to be "disciplined" for his failure to acquire this or that ability on time, he is also not to be prevented from learning to make an orderly and peaceful use of his time through being subjected to a spasmodic schedule of assignments. There is no reason why he should not have all his assignments given to him far enough ahead for him to plan to fulfill them systematically; he should not have two weeks of nothing much to do, followed by two weeks of altogether too much. This necessity means that there should be a coordination of the assignments by the faculty, one which gives the students due leisure and at least some chance to be trained in the use of it. It is true that in "real life" the student will not necessarily find that his tasks are nicely proportioned to his time and energy, and I am not here recommending that the scheduling of his work be done entirely for him; I am merely suggesting that in all fairness he be given a reasonable chance to be leisurely in meeting his personally determined "deadlines."

It is fairly clear from the discussion thus far that the ideal system of training would be tutorial. For in this system, the generating of enthusiasm, the getting down to fundamentals, the putting of the student through each process as his growth suggests, the freeing of the student from his fears, the gauging of his advancement without the use of frequent tests, the elimination therefore of useless testing and policing, the fair and helpful scheduling of assignments—all such matters could be taken care of with proper leisure for both student and teacher. This being so, I should like to suggest that if not freshmen and sophomores, then at least those juniors and seniors who have shown more than an ordinary interest in being educated be granted a tutorial training modelled somewhat on that of Oxford. If not this, then they could be granted a seminar training that will be in most, if not all respects, similar to that of our graduate schools.

In answer to the objection that there will not be time for us to do as much teaching as the tutorial or the seminar system require, I venture to say that time may be gained here in several ways. Let us resolve to teach only the vitally necessary arts and only the essentials of the sciences underlying these, being content to assure in the student that knowledge and skill which we would expect him to retain when he is ten years out of college. Let us reduce the number of outside activities over which we have to preside. Let us call upon our upper classmen to act as assistants in our freshmen and sophomore courses. Let us permit our students to relieve us of at least the routine disciplinary duties, the taking of attendance, and so on. Let us train all our students, through courses in the art of studying and through personal guidance, to do more and more work for themselves and call upon us for less and less mere lecturing. And let us give up once and for all such ideas as: that knowledge gulped down is true knowledge; that we must get through the book and may not digress into wisdom. If we must choose, and I do not think that we must, between turning out the half-educated man who has taken the time to learn facts but not the time to work out what they mean or to practice putting them to the best use, and the half-educated man who has had the time to master only a few basic facts and to understand what they mean and what to do with them, we must simply choose to turn out the second.

But whatever of these things we may or may not choose to do, one thing we must do: learn to cherish leisure as the prime requirement of all truly liberal education, for only that education is truly liberal (as Aristotle long ago pointed out in the *Metaphysics* and as Plato had pointed out before him in the *Laws*) in which the student is freed at least for the time being, from all need to get things done quickly, from all economic or political or personal concerns, so that he is free to listen, to discuss, to investigate, to practice, as if he had "all the time in the world," treating each new subject or skill as if it were exclusively an end in itself. Only in such an education is the student's mind sufficiently peaceful, sufficiently possessed of that "tranquility of order" which enables him to lose himself in his work as he should. And only an institution that assures him of such a peace-filled leisure deserves, as etymology tells us, the name of a place of leisure, the name *school*.

Author's Note:

In the course of the discussion which followed this talk, the author cited, as an excellent illustration of the principles set forth here and in the talks by Professor Nutting, the apprenticeship which was given to Shailer by Agassiz, as this is described in Chapter VII, "I Become Agassiz's Pupil at Harvard," of *The Autobiography of Nathaniel Southgate Shailer* (Houghton Mifflin, 1909). He also suggested as not unreasonable that some such experience be enjoyed by every student at least once in his career.

The passages in which Shailer describes his apprenticeship run as follows:—

"When I sat me down before my tin pan, Agassiz brought me a small fish, placing it before me with the rather stern requirement that I should study it, but on no account talk to anyone concerning it, nor read anything related to fishes, until I had permission to do so. To my inquiry, "What shall I do?" he said in effect: "Find out what you can without damaging the specimen; when I think you have done the work I will question you." In the course of an hour I thought I had compassed that fish; it was rather an unsavory object, giving forth the stench of old alcohol, then loathsome to me, though in time I came to like it. Many of the scales were loosened so that they fell off. It appeared to me to be a case for a summary report, which I was anxious to make and get on to the next stage of the business. But Agassiz, though always within call, concerned himself with me no further that day, nor the next, nor for a week. At first, this neglect was distressing; but I saw that it was a game, for he was, as I discerned rather than saw, covertly watching me. So I set my wits to work upon the thing, and in the course of a hundred hours or so thought I had done much—a hundred times as much as seemed possible at the start. I got interested in finding out how the scales went in series, their shape, the form and placement of the teeth, etc. Finally, I felt full of the subject and probably expressed it in my bearing; as for words about it then, there were none from my master except his cheery, "Good morning." At length, on the seventh day, came the question "Well?" and my disgorge of knowledge to him as he sat on the edge of my table puffing his cigar. At the end of the hour's telling, he swung off and away, saying, "That is not right." Here I began to think that after all the rules for scanning Latin verse were not the worst infliction in the world. Moreover, it was clear that he was playing a game with me to find if I were capable of doing hard, continuous work without the support of a teacher, and this stimulated me to labor. I went at the task anew, discarded my first notes, and in another week of ten hours a day labor I had results which astonished myself and satisfied him. Still there was no trace of praise in words or manner. He signified that it would do by placing before me about half a peck of bones, telling me to see what I could make of them, with no further directions to guide me. I soon found they were the skeletons of half a dozen fishes of different species; the jaws told me that much at a first inspection. The task evidently was to fit the separate bones together in their proper order. Two months or more went to this task with no other help than an occasional looking over my grouping with the stereotyped remark: "That is not right." Finally, the task was done and I was again set upon alcoholic specimens—this time a remarkable lot of specimens representing, perhaps, twenty species of the side-swimmers or *Pleuronectidae*. I shall never forget the sense of power in dealing with things which I felt in beginning the more extended work on a group of animals. I had learned the art of comparing objects, which is the basis of the naturalist's work. At this stage I was allowed to read and to discuss my work with others about me. I did both eagerly, and acquired a considerable knowledge of the literature of icthyology, becoming especially interested in the system of classification, then most imperfect. I tried to follow Agassiz's scheme of division into the order of ctenoids and ganoids, with the result that I found one of my species of side-swimmers had cycloid scales on one side and ctenoid on the other. This not only shocked my sense of the value of classification in a way that permitted of no full recovery of my original respect for the process, but for a time shook my confidence in my master's knowledge. At the same time I had a malicious pleasure in exhibiting my *find* to him, expecting to repay in part the humiliation which he had evidently tried to inflict on my conceit. To my question as to how the nondescript would be classified he said: "My boy, there are now two of us who know that."

This incident of the fish made an end of my novitiate. After that, with a suddenness of transition which puzzled me, Agassiz became very communicative; we passed indeed into the relation of friends of like age and purpose, and he actually consulted me as to what I should like to take up as a field of study.

. . . By far the greater part of the instruction I had from my master was in divers bits of talk concerning species and the arrangement of the specimens. He would often work with me for hours unrolling fossils, all the while keeping up a running commentary which would range this way and that, of men, of places, of Aristotle, of Oken. He was a perfect narrator, and on any peg of fact would quickly hang a fascinating discourse. Often when he was at work on wet specimens while I was dealing with fossils, he would come to me with, say, a fish in each hand, that I might search in his pockets for a cigar, cut the tip, put it between his teeth, and light it for him. That would remind him of something, and he would puff and talk until the cigar was burned out, and he would have to be provided with another.

. . . In my room my master became divinely young again. He would lie on the sofa, drink what I had to offer—I brought with me the then Southern habit of offering wine to guests—take a pipe and return in mind to his student days, or to his plans for work, or to his scheme of a museum which should present the animal and vegetable kingdoms so plainly that he who ran would perforce read—and deeply. I have never known a mind of such exuberance, of such eager contact with large desires. I was in thorough sympathy with this museum and with his projects, so that I had large profit from these interesting meetings, for they awakened an enthusiasm for constructive work which I doubt if any other accident of life would have aroused.

The meetings of the Zoological Club, at which all sorts of problems were discussed, were never attended by Agassiz. To our request that he would join us his answer was that we had better work alone, though he advised us to gather about us all who were interested in our problems, and to give our joint studies a wide range. I see now that while much concerned for our advancement, his aim was to have us stand alone, or at least to lean only on our mates. Although he could not help shaping those about him to his mode of thought, and was often indignant with them when they departed from his path, he had a sound practical sense of the danger of founding a school of followers; more than once he commented on this error of other masters."

. . . (A footnote): In Mr. Shailer's notebook for April 7, 1860, is this entry: "Professor Agassiz in his lecture this morning dwelt upon the requirements of a scientific man who would be more than a species-describer. The great test, he said, was to be able to deal with your subject in different ways. In amplifying the idea, he said it was well to be able to give in a single sentence the whole matter of months of labor, in a form so true that a scientific man could read in it not only the extent of your knowledge, but also the habit of your mind. He declared he could learn all this from an answer couched in the most laconic form. He said he should require of us in our several departments first a monograph, second a scientific lecture, third a popular lecture, fourth a simple child's tale."

Discipline and Unity of Atmosphere

By Hilary Martin, O.S.B.

The subject of our discussion this morning is Discipline and Unity of Atmosphere. We may, for our purpose, limit the term atmosphere to that mental and moral environment arising primarily from the visual arts in all their extension.

As Catholics, we may at once affirm the fact that art is not the business of the Church, any more than politics or economics. Even less, some would say. The business of the Church we know is the making of saints. Only in so far as art (or politics or economics) may lead to or prevent the making of the saint, is she properly interested. As Eric Gill has pointed out,[1] it is not the business of the Church or her ministers to dictate to builders or to any other kind of artists, except to the same degree as any good customer can impose certain qualifications on work he may commission. Nor did churchmen do more, except in certain extraordinary cases, in the mediaeval period, when the external expression of Christianity reached its apogee. The culture was Catholic at that time, but only in the sense that the under-lying ideas of society were Catholic, not that it was a direct product of the Church or ecclesiastics. The supremacy of the Church in matters of faith and morals does not destroy the autonomy of man as an artist any more than it does man as a politician.

You, as educators, are concerned in art in the sense that you are involved in what is an aesthetic process, "a succession of problem, solution and execution."[2] You are, however, concerned in art in a more restricted meaning, since you are necessarily in a position of sanctioning, at least tacitly, architecture, sculpture, and painting, as it appears in all the structures given over to education in the institutions you represent. I am not implying that, as individuals, you have commissioned the buildings in which you may

---
[1] Eric Gill, *Beauty Looks After Herself* (New York: Sheed and Ward, 1933), p. 31.
[2] A. K. Coomaraswamy, *The Transformation of Nature in Art* (Cambridge, Mass.: Harvard University Press), p. 64.

teach or in which your students may eat, sleep, play, study, or worship, but, whether you are responsible for your own surroundings or not is immaterial. What is important is for you to become conscious of the effect these surroundings may have on those whom you are seeking to educate, since it contributes to the impressions they receive and cannot but affect their mentalities; and being conscious, that you recognize the importance of this influence.

May I re-assure you that I am not advocating "Art for Art's Sake," but rather art for God's sake. As Christian educators you are primarily concerned with the leading of youths into a Christian mentality. It is obvious that we can contribute far more to the demoralization of youth than to their education by an important inconsistency in the framework of the educative process. We may, for example, lecture until hoarse on the heroic attitude necessary for the contemporary Christian in a secular world and demonstrate intellectually how all heroism is contained in Christ. Our work will be subtly but nonetheless quite thoroughly undermined, however, by what those same students see. We say that Christ is the epitome of heroism, but permit Him to be shown as weak and effeminate, His only recognizable claim to virility being a chocolate beard. Or else we may, by many means, seek to inculcate in students the ideals of Christian modesty and dignity embodied in the Mother of God, who has been described as "terrible as an army in array." If, however, the Virgin is portrayed with characteristics which seem to be more closely allied to a vegetable than to the Queen of Heaven, our efforts will, to say the least, be vitiated.

We cannot neglect any activity of the human soul and hope to achieve that integration in Christ which is the Christian vocation. The heavenly Jerusalem can only be reached by progress through the earthly Jerusalem, and this latter is filled with many human activities, one of which is art. In our contemporary concern with the practical order of the virtues of the mind, we should not forget the one which is closest, from many points of view, to the speculative. Too many of us agree, if only tacitly, with Leon Bloy, that art is an aboriginal parasite on the skin of the first serpent. This is not a reflection of our religion, unless we be Jansenists. Nor can we justify our attitude, as can Bloy his extravagance, as serving only to illustrate the profound antimony which may occur in any profound activity of the human soul. We are, if not slightly scornful, what is worse, indifferent, or woefully inadequate in approaching this activity, which has such an important contribution to make to the education of youth.

We are not here concerned with discussing the producing of Catholic artists. I believe that if we produce Catholics the artists will take care of themselves. Art springs from the contemporary culture. If our culture can be infused with the spirit of Christianity, then our artists will do the works of Christ. What we are concerned with is to remedy the contradiction which I have briefly touched upon above, namely, teaching the value of the Christian virtues and then denying them, not in the moral example of our lives, but in the physical example of our institutions. This is not to say that we should all become architects, painters, and sculptors. It does, however, require a certain rational approach to all of the matters concerning these visual arts.

I do not know why people can be intelligently humble in approaching the profession of medicine, while at the same time, they blithely rush into the fields of the architect, sculptor, and painter with an assurance that is incredible. It may be, perhaps, because a mistake in medicine may bring with it an illness, even loss of life itself, while a mistake in other fields is considered an interesting bit of self-expression, and hence an experience to be sought avidly. Whatever it is, the relative importance of errors in these fields may be summed up in the old saying: a doctor buries his mistakes, while all an architect can do is plant a vine. In other words, poor judgment in medicine does not normally perpetuate itself for generations as it does in the arts, particularly architecture.

What I am making a plea for is, of course, the natural virtue of humility. That, I believe, is the most important quality for any person approaching any of the arts. And the fact that all our friends assure us that what we have is called good taste is no indication that we are qualified to make decisions belonging to the professional alone. Personal taste is no guarantee of sound judgment unless it be supported by knowledge, and knowledge of art does not consist in either a course in that branch of philosophy called aesthetics, nor in a course in the history of art. We must recognize that professional qualifications involve in the arts, just as they do in other professions, years of concentrated study and years of practice. The amateur in any of these fields is a menace, not only to his fellow man, but perhaps to countless generations yet unborn. You should not have to look far to verify these words.

That we may not be professionals in these fields is no reason, however, why we should not be able to acquire a point of view which would make us handle intelligently problems related to the arts. I cannot hope to give you that point of view this morning. It is a matter of education in the broadest sense of that term, requiring research, study, and a great deal of that process called meditation. I would like, however, to suggest to you certain thoughts in connection with the field with which I am most familiar, that of architecture.

When, in the early seventeenth century, Sir Henry Wotton adapted Vitruvius' "Elements of Architecture," he phrased the Augustan architect's dictum thus: "Well-building hath three conditions: Commodity, Firmness, Delight." Through the demands of "Firmness," architecture is related to science. Physics, statics, and dynamics suggest and control the structural elements and justify their relationship. "Commodity" ties it to human life since architecture satisfies a human need. Hence, religious, political, social, economic, and racial factors are elements which must receive their proper expression. "Delight" is the result of the disinterested desire for beauty, a desire that does not culminate in a purely aesthetic result, since Commodity has imposed utilitarian demands, but is rather an aesthetic impulse which effects the metamorphosis of the science into the art. These then are the conditions upon which architecture depends. While it cannot be asserted that there exists a principle of pre-established harmony between them, it should be evident that any serious deordination can result only in a negation of well-building. The question of the concessions which science must make to art, or art to science and utility, can never be answered. It is in the satisfactory solution of the conditions imposed by each, in compromise, that true architecture may be found.

In this country, architecture has at long last come of age. From the earliest times we have sought on the other side of the Atlantic the vocabulary with which to express ourselves. All our styles of building have arrived on this shore completely articulate, and, if we have made some of them our own, the indigenous elements with which they have been modified have been accidental, not basic. The achievements of men like Louis Sullivan, Frank Lloyd Wright, and the creators of such complete expressions as the Rockefeller Center in New York, however, leave nothing wanting in the conditions of well-building.

In the R.C.A. Building a structure has been produced which is as significant and as expressive of our culture as the broad domes of Byzantium and the soaring gothic towers of the Middle Ages were for theirs. In commercial structure particularly has America expressed herself best—best because what is closest to the heart most easily finds expression in art. There is, however, an extraordinary lag between the embodiment of our commercial achievements and that of our faith. Who can point out a contemporary church which so satisfies the requisites of architecture as does the R.C.A. Building? It is this tragic condition that I would briefly analyse, in order to indicate wherein those who build such superb expressions of commercial achievement fail so pitifully when they turn to construct a house of God. For the error lies in the minds of us all: we think clearly enough when both the immediate and ultimate ends are utilitarian, but when the latter end is of the spirit our wisdom leaves by one window, our knowledge by another, and so with all the seven gifts, until there remains but the hollow shell inhabited by a few spectres and taboos which determine wherein we shall worship God.

In turning to contemporary American churches let us once and for all kill the vicious excuse that we are, or were but lately, a missionary country, that the practical problems of our Church were so great that such an "amenity" as architecture could not in justice be expected, or even hoped for. This vampire can be buried at the cross-roads and the essential stake driven quietly through its heart by turning to our Southwest and California. There, in a truly missionary country, in the midst of a rude people and with very limited means, the Franciscans built churches whose Commodity, Firmness, and Delight set standards as yet unsurpassed in this country. Where then do we fail?

We despise Firmness. Our usual church building either denies the contributions of contemporary science which suggest and justify a contemporary disposition of structural elements, or else perverts these achievements, calling them in to serve merely in making up for the deficiencies and in supporting the extravagances of out-moded building methods. Only in an age when Hollywood is not merely the center of an industry, but threatens to succeed the Academy of Athens, the Universities of Bologna and Padua, of Paris and Oxford as the fount of culture, could a flying buttress be constructed of reinforced concrete. It is not coincidence that the baroque mathematician was working with the infinite as a basis for his calculations at the same time as the architect was employing the impression of infinity as an artistic effect. The universalistic point of view of that time resulted simultaneously in the integral calculus and in that union of geometry with imagination which characterized the genius of Borromini, of Guarini, of Balthasar Neumann and the rest. We cannot shun or enfeeble, or, still worse, pervert science and produce architecture.

And how do we regard Commodity? How are the social, economic, and racial factors reflected in the design of our churches? How accurately is our culture portrayed in these buildings, and how well do they fulfill the utilitarian demands of the Liturgy? A cathedral purporting to be Gothic provides a humiliating contrast with the indigenous architecture just across Fifth Avenue. Another employing the vocabulary of Byzantium and Provence seeks to express the ethos of the great Mississippi and Missouri River valleys—but one might continue down almost the whole list of large American churches. All expression of culture disdained, the utilitarian demands are scarcely better satisfied. Too often do the plans of our churches reflect either a liturgical ambition far beyond any possible realization, or they go to the other extreme and present a scheme of peculiar liturgical impotency. The choir is in a gallery at the opposite end of the nave from the High Altar which is removed as far as possible from those assisting at the function which is taking place upon it. The High Altar is subjected to the indignity of having its pre-eminence threatened by the presence of a number of other altars, whose sole function seems to be, in most cases, to act as repositories for candlesticks and flower vases placed before indifferent representations of saints. The regulations laid down wisely by the Church herself are flagrantly disobeyed. And seldom is the church itself planned as a part of an integral scheme whose varied educational, social, and residential functions must be maintained, if the church is to occupy her effective place in the community.

As for Delight, that condition which raises the practical ends and their mechanical solutions to the dignity of an art, in our church buildings it usually founders on the sunken reefs of Romanticism, which is inimical to practical, philosophic, and scientific achievement and is, above all, antipathetic to a true conception of plastic forms. Being essentially poetic, its best expression may be found it literature and music, but under its spell the interest in architecture runs to the symbolic, and stylistic, and the antiquarian, detail coming to be regarded as the supreme consideration instead of the ancillary factor it is. "We must have a Gothic church, it's such a spiritual style," or "Let us return to the builders of the Ages of Faith," are two ways grown-ups have of enjoying what children call "playing house." They will not return to the spirit of the Gothic builders or to that of the builders of any other age, but will only nibble at the lotus of Romanticism and sink into that lovely region of make-believe where Sunday morning must be Romanesque or Byzantine or Gothic or whatever you like as long as it does not belong to today, while the architectural setting of the other six mornings of the week must be in a style that is at least two steps ahead of tomorrow. The result is that our churches at best are not architectural but aesthetic, since the desire for beauty has culminated in a mere artistic effect rather than in an impulse which would have carried forward the solution of the problems of Commodity and Firmness into the realms of creative art.

It may be of some slight consolation, where none, it must be admitted, is deserved, that this indictment of contemporary church building is in this country equally just in respect to churches erected by those professing creeds other than our own. Mr. Rockefeller, who must share some responsibility in giving us the superb group of structures in New York that bear his name, shows, in turning his hand to the problem of church building, the emotionalism of any contemporary church building committee and has blotted Riverside Drive with as unhappy an expression of the builder's craft as may be found in that remarkable hunting ground.

The indictment then seems true of American church building in general rather than Catholic church building in particular, when we regard the work of our co-religionists in Central Europe in that period between 1920 and 1935. During those years of reconstruction, hundreds of Catholic churches were built, many of which can claim to have met the demands of Firmness, Commodity, and Delight. From the great industrial cities of the Rhineland to the villages lost in the plains of Hungary and the valleys of Bavaria and Switzerland, have risen churches large and small which share in the scientific zeal for constructive evolution which marked the Gothic period, which share also to some extent in the creative vigor of the Renascence and reflect to the fullest our own age and its philosophy. For an architecture must reflect the philosophy of the age in which it is evolved. We have seen that a baroque mathematics was being developed along with a baroque architecture. In an earlier period it was no accident that the invention of perspective, which made possible the architectural conceptions of the Renascence, coincided with the development of individualism as the touchstone of the new humanism. Does the answer lie in this: that the prevailing philosophy of our people is so completely pragmatic that we are capable of transforming the demands of commerce into art but those of religion only into aestheticism? Those involved in Catholic education had better face the task that is here presented to them.

Please do not misunderstand what I have just said as an apology for all contemporary expression in the visual arts. There is all too evident a preference for novelty, the illusion of an era dominated as ours is by the natural sciences in which the new fact is continually replacing the old. Besides this, the intention of the contemporary artist is all too often not the expression of his object, but of himself. The egocentricity of our time can hardly be better seen than in the example of an internationally famous painter who has completely altered his technique so frequently that his work is catalogued as belonging to various "periods," illustrating that his intention is self-expression rather than that which he apprehends, that which possesses him and is then expressed. Contemporary art in all of its forms must be approached with a great deal of caution, not only because of the peculiarities mentioned above, but also because it is naturally more difficult for us to recognize what is good and what is spurious, lacking, as we do, the perspective of time so necessary even for experts to form a sound judgment.

Nor am I suggesting that we abandon tradition. What we should seek from the past is not so much a heritage of forms but one of mentality. We should endeavor to achieve a restatement of transcendental truth, a restatement which was so effectively done in another field, for example, by St. Augustine. What differentiates the Gothic from the Romanesque, and both of them from the Renascence and the baroque, is not so much the forms but the varying aspirations of each. Forms are fundamentally an effect of what is called a style, not a cause.

We may illustrate a case of the contemporary poverty of mind in this regard by referring to the present so-called restoration of Monte Cassino. The basilica of that monastery has been rebuilt four times before this, in the Eighth, Tenth, Eleventh and during the Sixteenth and Seventeenth Centuries. Never was it "restored" in the sense in which that term is now used. Each time the builders expressed their culture in the contemporary vernacular without, however, disdaining the traditions of their predecessors. One of the most interesting restorations was that in the Eleventh Century under the Abbot Desiderius, who later became Pope Victor the Third. In spite of strong local Greek traditions, he returned to the form of the Constantinian basilica prevalent in Italy centuries before. However, there were obvious differences, both in plan and in the relationship of spatial elements which were truly original and provided an inspiration for countless church buildings in Italy and as far away as Burgundy.

A contrast to the restoration of Monte Cassino, but not a much happier one, is seen in certain contemporary church buildings here as well as abroad. The modern worship of function as a primary end crossed with the modern love of novelty has resulted in what may be called an unhappy offspring of highly questionable parentage. It is a mistake to think that everything must be reduced to what performs a useful function. This is true of machinery or such embodiments of mechanism as the automobile, the ship, and the airplane. While art does not consist in decoration, it permits appropriate decoration. Fenelon once said, "No part of a building should be there merely as a decoration. The architect, aiming always at beautiful proportions, should rather make decorative every part necessary for supporting a building." The obsession with function, like any other human aberation, however, defeats its purpose when limited by the physical requirements of religious worship. The architect can then only give us a building in which the spirit, the vehicle of religion, is completely thwarted. The building may function physically, but so does a well laid-out super-market.

I have treated at some little length a few of the problems and principles connected with architecture, but nothing should be beyond our interest and consideration in the field of any of the arts. "Art is a functional necessity in the human state," says Jacques Maritain,[3] and he admirably demonstrates the truth of this statement, a demonstration I would recommend to you to follow. It is particularly true that we should be vitally concerned with any reproductions of Christian subjects whether in stone or plaster, paint or printer's ink. As Charlton Fortune [4] says, "For a very long time we have accepted weak and mediocre presentations of Christ and Our Lady without criticism, because of the subjects they attempt to portray. This has come about because of our misunderstanding of the function of art." Or, I would add, a misunderstanding of art in relation to man and religion.

Beyond all these direct considerations of art, however, we have the endless problems presented to us almost daily: the typography used in our school catalogues and announcements, the colors used on the walls of our educational institutions, and so on *ad infinitum*. In regard to this last

---

[3] Jacques Maritain, *Art and Scholasticism* (New York: Charles Scribner, 1930), p. 80.
[4] Charlton Fortune, *Notes on Art for Catholics* (Paterson, N. J.: St. Anthony's Guild Press, 1944), p. 9.

category in particular, I would suggest that we endeavor to get away from the pastry kitchen. We have, at least in most places, freed ourselves from the peanut brittle of the Victorians, an age whose culture could hardly be described as Christian, only to fall in with the so-called moderns, whose limits seem to be pistachio and raspberry.

I would rather not mention at all the subject of holy cards and so called church calendars. The former usually are limited in their sentimentality only by their rather restricted size; the latter perform their function of giving us certain information as to time, when we may not eat meat and when we must attend Mass, only under a welter of sickly representation which some times verges on the scandalous.

Religion does not depend on externals, but can it be divorced from life except in extraordinary circumstances and retain its vitality? In neglecting the outward expression of Christianity are we not encouraging the very tendency we deplore, of establishing in life a fatal dichotomy? The division of life into compartments, one marked "Sunday morning only," is a tendency in our time of which we are all too well aware. As educators can we neglect any means to help those sent to us for their formation in achieving that integration of their lives in Christ, which is the only proper end of any effort on our part or on theirs?

Discipline and Asceticism

By Edmond Darvil Benard

I suspect that when the officers of the Workshop assigned to this lecture the title, "Discipline and Asceticism," they did so with full advertence to its provocative—one might almost say, hazardous—sound. It would be difficult indeed to find two words more calculated than "discipline" and "asceticism" to irritate the self-consciously enlightened and the less consciously sentimental educator. To those unaware of their ignorance of its meaning, "asceticism" conjures up a picture of a haggard eremite, lightly garbed in what is certainly not an academic robe, and residing in a desert cave whose decorative *motif* is a gruesome and probably unsanitary skull. "Discipline" is thought of by the historically minded as symbolized in the eighteenth century New England schoolmaster's birch rod; by the literary-minded according to their vague memories of *Nicholas Nickleby;* and by the fanciful in terms of the Duchess' song:

> Speak roughly to your little boy,
> And beat him when he sneezes;
> He only does it to annoy,
> Because he knows it teases.

Such ideas are not, I am well aware, shared by the members of this Workshop. But discipline is at best a difficult subject; and no one would dare to say, I hope, that Catholic educators have never made or do not now sometimes make mistakes regarding its concept, its application, and its relationship to other elements of scholastic life. As students we have sometimes observed, or at least thought we observed, such mistakes; as teachers we have, perhaps, been responsible for them.

Now good discipline in an educational institution implies both sound principles and their intelligent application. This paper is concerned mainly with the first element—certain basic principles. The judgment as to their soundness and the details of their application are left to the members of the Workshop. As a further limitation, we are concerned immediately with the relationships between discipline and what we call the ascetical life. I hasten to admit that what I have to say is based upon theory and observation, not on personal experience of responsibility; I have never been entrusted with the disciplinary problems of any institution, nor have I ever been consulted with regard to them. Perhaps this is the only reason why I was able to begin this paper in rather a light vein. "He jests at scars that never felt a wound." But if theory is well-founded, it will result in sound practice, even though the practice will inevitably be conditioned by the particular circumstances of the *milieu* in which it is exercised. I have a further admission to make. In preparation for this lecture, I applied myself grimly to the reading of a number of treatises on education by authors, some Catholic, some non-Catholic. The fault is undoubtedly mine, but I found that while the individual words used by many distinguished professional educators seem clear enough, the meaning of their combinations in sentences often escapes me. To quote the most inappropriate poet possible for a lecture on asceticism:

> Myself when young did eagerly frequent
> Doctor and Saint, and heard great argument
>   About it and about: but evermore
> Came out by that same door where in I went.

With these preliminary apologies a matter of record, we may now proceed to the business before the house.

Some Definitions

In order to understand the relationships between discipline and asceticism, we must first make clear what is meant by the terms employed. Let us be as brief as possible.

Discipline is taken here in its general sense as signifying *authoritative direction*. The *direction* involved applies both to learning and living, i.e., both curriculum and conduct. It implies the existence and promulgation of rules that can be easily understood and that make up a reasonable norm. The direction is *authoritative* because it includes clear and just sanctions and because it is to be respected and obeyed. This notion will be further developed in the course of the paper, but it will suffice here as a preliminary idea.

The word "asceticism" comes from the Greek *áskesis,* which means exercise, practice, training. The ascetical life, then, means for us the striving for the attainment of Christian perfection. When we deal with asceticism, we deal simply with the correct use of the means given us by God for advancement in His knowledge and love. It is true that the word is frequently given a much more limited sense, as applying to a life of self-denial and to the practice of various works of mortification. But we make no such limitation in this paper. The ascetical training given in a Catholic college is the training given in total Christian living, with the aim being the formation of genuine Christian (which is to say, Christ-like) character. This general sense of the word "asceticism," it might be mentioned, is the sense employed by Pope Pius XII in the Encyclical *Mediator Dei.*

The question with which our discussion deals thus resolves itself to this: what are the relationships between authoritative direction and the formation of genuine Christian character in the students of a Catholic college? This is a question that has a number of different aspects and is patient of various angles of approach. I think that we can pass over with very few words the problem of discipline as involved in curricular direction. Catholic colleges have always been eminently sane in their approach to electivism and have refused to regard their catalogues as bargain basements in which the student is absolutely free to select what he thinks he wants or needs and leave the rest. If a student wishes to gain an A.B. degree, he is obliged to pass the courses required for that degree. He may specialize, naturally, in a certain field within the limits of the A.B. and is free to select the courses useful for his specialization. The same thing is true of other degrees and of the fields of specialization within their orbits. But there is a genuine curricular discipline, an authoritative guidance and direction. We may pass over also the question of discipline as concerned with the mere maintenance of classroom order. This is seldom a problem in college, and it is fair to say that it is never a problem when the matter of the class lectures is carefully prepared and interestingly presented.

Having eliminated with a brief reference the relationship of discipline and curriculum, we can now devote ourselves to the question of discipline and conduct; or, in other words, the relationship of authoritative direction and the life of the Catholic college community.

Means and End

Since the end to be gained specifies and determines the means to be employed, the attributes of a genuine Christian character will specify and determine the type of discipline that should be characteristic of the Catholic college.

The first thing to be remarked about discipline, then, is precisely that it *is* a means and *not* an end in itself. When the rule of a college acquires a quasi-deification so that obedience to regulations is presented as a high good sufficient unto itself, then all sense of proportion has been lost.

Perhaps those of us who are members of religious orders, or who have received seminary training, are sometimes prone to attach too much importance to the rule-in-itself. Members of a religious community should not identify the regulations of the college they conduct with the holy rule to which they have vowed obedience as a religious act. The rule of a religious order has been selected by its members as a permanent, life-long guide and safeguard; but the disciplinary regulations of a college will not guide and protect the students for as long as they shall live, but only during their four-year term as undergraduates. The function of college discipline, the function of the rule of student conduct, is to form in the students habits of self-discipline that will persist when the rule-in-itself is only a memory of college days. The college rule is respected and obeyed not precisely for what it is, but for what it does. It is not an end, but a means to an end.

Closely allied to the idolization of the rule-in-itself is the attitude of certain college disciplinarians who seem determined that college shall be a prolongation of adolescense rather than the inception of adulthood. There is a tendency among present-day psychologists to abandon the definition of "adolescence" in terms of the psycho-physical changes of puberty and to catalogue it rather according to its social or sociological aspect. Thus "adolescence" would be described broadly as the period in which the youth has an ambivalent relationship to family and community and is the object of an ambiguous attitude on the part of his elders. Concretely, he is regarded both as a boy and as a man. He is appealed to as a man; he is ruled as a boy. He is often *held* responsible for his actions as a man but is *given* responsibility only as a boy. The adolescent himself demands to be trusted and treated as a man, but he frequently seeks to escape the consequence of his actions on the ground of his boyhood. And both the adolescent and his elders are tempted to appeal to alternate terms of the boy-man equation as it suits their purposes to do so.

Now it is inevitable that the element of adolescence should complicate the disciplinary problem and regulations of a high school; but surely college discipline should be predicated on the ability and readiness of the student to be treated primarily as an adult. This means, I think, that disciplinary regulations should be presented with full explanation of their individual and social necessity and value; they should be so presented that they are respected and accepted for what they *do,* not for what they *are;* they should be presented as means to a worthwhile goal, not as an end in themselves; they should be explained with emphasis on their positive benefits, not upon their negative sanction. A large measure of personal responsibility for their observance should be entrusted to the student, with a minimum of administrative "checking-up." Surely it is unwise to treat a college student as a child for four years and then expect him to be ready to live an adult life through some mechanical commencement day magic.

Christian Character

Since discipline is a means, it is specified by its end; and we have seen that the end of Catholic education—an end which coalesces with the end of the ascetical life—is the formation of the genuine Christian character. This character has been described for us by Pope Pius XI in his Encyclical Letter on the Christian Education of Youth:

. . . the true Christian, product of Christian education, is the supernatural man who thinks, judges and acts constantly and consistently in accordance with right reason illumined by the supernatural light of the example and teaching of Christ; in other words, to use the current term, the true and finished man of character....

The true Christian does not renounce the activities of this life, he does not stunt his natural faculties; but he develops and perfects them, by co-ordinating them with the supernatural. He thus enobles what is merely natural in life and secures for it new strength in the material and temporal order, no less than in the spiritual and eternal.[1]

It is clear from these words of Pope Pius XI that the graduate of a Catholic college should have (1) a true sense of values, of proportion, a firm conviction of the primacy of the supernatural, a *real* and vital persuasion of the truth of Our Lord's question: "What doth it profit a man if he gain the whole world, and suffer the loss of his own soul?" He should have (2) a genuine respect for, and *desire* to be guided by the law of God above all, and consequently by the legitimate laws derived from that eternal one; and he should be informed in his every action by the summary of the law and the prophets which Christ promulgated both by teaching and example: the two great commandments of love of God and of neighbor. He should have (3) a real coördination of natural faculties with the supernatural. These attributes of the Christian character will be our guide in the consideration of some aspects of college discipline.

Discipline and the Sense of Values

If the supernatural is of prime importance in any sound hierarchy of values, the disciplinary rule of the Catholic college must reflect and stress this importance. Are our colleges to be Catholic or are they not? If they are, then the rule of college life must take for granted the importance of the spiritual exercises in the daily, weekly, and monthly college program. Let us take a single example.

It has been my impression that in few Catholic colleges are the students really persuaded that morning Mass is just as completely and thoroughly an item of their college day as is, for instance, the nine o'clock class in English literature.

---

[1] N. C. W. C. edition (Washington, D. C., 1936), pp. 36-37.

And yet, if we are to have any concern for the ascetical life—for the search for Christian perfection—is there a better habit that could be inculcated in the student than the habit of daily Mass?

I am not at all sure that the growing custom in Catholic colleges of making the attendance at daily Mass completely optional is a good thing. I am aware of all the arguments that can be advanced: there must be no "compulsion" in spiritual things; students "get no good out of" a Mass they are "forced" to attend, etc., etc., etc. I would not presume to dictate to a particular college just what is the best method in its particular circumstances to encourage the custom of daily attendance at Mass. But this I can say: if there is a Catholic college where only a small proportion of the student body (of the resident students at least) attend daily Mass, *there is something wrong with that college.* If discipline is authoritative guidance in true Christian living, then the discipline in that college is a rather futile thing.

On this point of discipline and the primacy of the supernatural, I should like to make one other remark—from a psychological viewpoint. It deals with the association of ideas. (I might state, parenthetically, that I am not going to enter into the controversy on the "conditioned reflex." Pavlov's dog may bark, but *this* caravan passes on.)

It is certainly true that a good thing may be made distasteful if it is associated with a disagreeable thing. Hence, one of the worst mistakes that a Catholic college disciplinarian could make would be to connect up a spiritual practice with an arbitrarily disagreeable circumstance.

Now obviously I do not mean that the ascetical life can be separated from a salutary element of self-denial. For instance, if a student is to attend Mass, he must rise before the bell for breakfast. But I do mean, for example, the practice of a certain Catholic girls' college disciplinarian of assigning a compulsory period of prayer in chapel as punishment for a minor infraction of the rules of the school. Is there any better way of provoking in the unfortunate student a distaste for visiting the Blessed Sacrament than to make such a visit a penalty? The intentions of the disciplinarian are certainly pious and good; but pious and good intentions can lead to definite psychological blunders.

Discipline and the Desire for Law

Bishop John Lancaster Spalding, in an address at the Catholic University of America, once said: "Rules and laws are of little use to those who have not been brought up to desire and love the guidance of law." [2] We must remember, as has already been pointed out, that the disciplinary regulations of a college are not to be a permanent rule of life for the students: after four years they will not longer be subject to the letter of its positive demands and negative restrictions. If college discipline is to play a positive and lasting role in the formation of Christian character, it must be so organized, explained, and presented that the habits it helps to form will become enduring character-traits in the college graduates. Our college rules must further the desire and love of law, and not, by their arbitrary character, foster disrespect for law. A college rule honored more in the breach than the observance is worse than no law at all. I have in mind the case, brought to my attention a short time ago, of a college where, by regulation, resident students are forbidden to keep automobiles at school. No cars are parked on campus, true: but I have been reliably informed that there are few unrented garages in the neighborhood—and that it is not unknown for members of the faculty to enlist the services of student chauffeurs. Why not eliminate the prohibition?

Is it not possible, in an orientation course at the beginning of the student's college career, to present the disciplinary regulations of the college in such a fashion that their reasonable nature will be appreciated and their positive value as specific determinations—however remote—of the eternal divine law and the natural law be understood? This presupposes, of course, that the regulations are neither arbitrary nor superfluous. The college is a miniature community, and the student has just as much right to expect reasonable and just college regulations as he has to expect reasonable and just federal and state laws and city ordinances. The so-called "good disciplinarian" who conducts the discipline of a college mainly by force of personality is by no means an unmixed blessing. He or

---

[2] *Opportunity and Other Essays and Addresses* (Chicago: A. C. McClurg & Co., 1900), p. 119.

she may be able to maintain order in the college; but I very much doubt whether, when the student is no longer under such excessively personal jurisdiction, lasting habits of respect and desire for reasonable law will persist as a character-trait.

Natural and Supernatural

We have already referred to the function of college discipline in the formation of habits. This deserves, I think, consideration in some detail.

When we speak of habits in relation to action, we are, of course, dealing with what are called "operative habits." An operative habit may be defined as a "stable disposition which determines a faculty to operate badly or well." (Such "operative habits" are referred to in this paper simply as "habits.") We are familiar with "good" and "bad" habits. For example, temperance, which means specifically a reasonable moderation in matters of food and drink, is a good habit, while intemperance is a bad one. Both good and bad habits are acquired and strengthened by repeated acts. And in the acquisition and strengthening of good habits, which are customary modes of action that accord with right reason and divine law, there must be sound principles at the basis of the acts. It is a melancholy truth that bad habits are easier to acquire than good ones. This is because good habits are the result of self-control—control of man's lower nature by his higher faculties of intellect and will, a control that becomes progressively easier and more pleasant as the habit is more firmly rooted. Bad habits, on the other hand, betoken a lack of control of man's lower tendencies; they can readily become our masters by the simple process of our "letting ourselves go."

I do not think that anyone would quarrel with the statement that an essential function of college discipline is to assist the student in the formation of good habits and in the conquest of bad ones. And this essential function helps us to determine some characteristics of good discipline.

First of all, character training is primarily self-training. Good habits cannot be imposed by force. The students must know why the habits are good, he must want to acquire them, and he must be willing to persevere in the ascetical process that will develop and strengthen them. As long as actions are merely the result of an unquestioning subjection to specific orders, without an understanding of the underlying principles, they are almost valueless as far as the acquisition of life-long habits is concerned. An iron-clad rule that treats the students like children, for whom the simple word "because" is considered a sufficient reason, may keep them technically "innocent"; but as Cardinal Newman wrote, innocence without principle is hardly virtue.[3] "Do this because the rule of this college says so" is an extremely poor reason; and "do this because I, the college disciplinarian, say so" is even worse.

College discipline must not depend on commands and ukases if it is to develop good habits; it must concentrate principally on creating an environment in which the acquisition of good habits is natural and easy. The repeated acts that develop good habits must be encouraged by the college rule, and the acts that develop and manifest bad habits must find an uncongenial atmosphere. In this way college discipline can help the student train himself to virtue, instead of implicitly treating him as a prisoner under temporary and arbitrary restraint. And this mention of virtue leads us to the specific consideration of habits as they are related to the truly Christian life.

The supernatural life and the natural life are not two separate and discordant things. Grace perfects nature, it builds upon nature, it elevates and divinizes nature, but it does not destroy it. In the natural order, a man has a principle of life, the soul. The soul operates through faculties, which are perfected in their operation by good habits. In the supernatural order, grace is the principle of life, and grace operates through the virtues, which correspond to both faculties and habits in the natural order.

I think a close study of the magnificent theological treatise on the virtues would make rewarding reading for those concerned with the work of college discipline. Obviously, within the limits of this paper, not even a summary of the treatise can be attempted. But one salient point must be mentioned in illustration of the close connection between

---

[3] Cf. *My Campaign in Ireland*. Part I. Catholic University Reports and Other Papers. Printed for Private Circulation Only (Aberdeen: A. King & Co., 1896), p. 116.

discipline and asceticism, which is to say, let me remind my hearers again, the conection between authoritative direction and the formation of Christian character.

The acts of the Christian life which are the outward manifestation of Christian character are acts of virtue. When the gift of sanctifying grace—the supernatural life-principle—is bestowed upon the soul by God, He infuses at the same time the virtues by which grace becomes operative in our actions. The theological virtues of faith, hope, and charity; and the moral virtues summarized in the "cardinal virtues" of prudence, justice, temperance, and fortitude are given to us by God in this fashion, so that our actions may truly be "virtuous" in the strict supernatural sense of the word.

Now the infused moral virtues give us the *power* to perform good actions that are elevated to the status of acts of supernatural virtue; but it is obvious, from sad human experience, that they do not, at least in the beginning, give us *facility* in performing those actions. Take, for example, the case of a man who has been accustomed to cheat and steal at every opportunity; who has never been firmly convinced, by instruction, example, and environment, that honesty really is the best policy. He is converted from sin, makes a good confession, receives the gift of sanctifying grace with its concomitant infused virtue of justice. In spite of this infused virtue, at the first temptation to cheat or take unjust advantage of someone, the dead weight of the vice of injustice which he has spent a life-time solidifying will push him strongly towards the abyss of sin. Note that I do not say he will inevitably succumb to the temptation. No, God gives him sufficient grace to conquer the temptation, and if he really wills to cooperate with that grace, all will be well. But the struggle will be a tremendous one. A bad acquired habit will be at war with the infused virtue. The man will have the supernatural power to perform an act of justice, but he will lack the natural facility to do so.

Is it not evident that an important function of discipline is to aid in the acquisition of the good habits that are the natural counterparts of the supernatural virtues? Since the ascetical life that is the constant striving for Christian perfection is demonstrated by the performance of virtuous actions, is there not a close, very close relationship between discipline and asceticism? The perfect Christian operative mechanism is possessed when the soul is equipped with the infused virtues, rooted in grace, "informed" by charity, and guided by supernatural prudence, *plus* the *acquired* moral virtues which make the *exercise* of virtuous acts delightful, and joyful, and easy—the normal, customary thing to do.

Catholic college discipline cannot infuse virtues; that, God alone can do. But Catholic college discipline can play a momentous part in the formation of Christian character through its training in, and insistence upon, those repeated acts which create and strengthen the good habits that furnish facility in Christian living.

Conclusion

This paper has been concerned with some basic ideas on the nature of Catholic college discipline and its relationship to the formation of Christian character. I do not think that it is necessary to give a point-by-point summary of a treatment that has been in itself a summary. I do think, however, that a word should be said in conclusion concerning the manner in which discipline is exercised and applied. We have criticized the mis-named "good disciplinarian" who rules by mere force of personality and not according to a recognized and reasonable code. The real "good disciplinarian" is one who uses prudence and charity, as well as justice, *in the enforcement of the code*. And this is a high art which is to be approached in humility and exercised in patience and prayer. In an outline of "Rules and Regulations" which John Henry Newman, then rector of the Catholic University of Ireland, submitted to his council in April, 1856, we find a picture of Catholic college discipline. It is the duty and privilege of Catholic college disciplinarians, Newman wrote, to conduct their students

> . . . to the arms of a kind mother, an Alma Mater, who inspires affection while she whispers truth; who enlists imagination, taste, and ambition on the side of duty; who seeks to impress hearts with noble and heavenly maxims at the age when they are most susceptible, and to win and subdue them when they are most impetuous and self-willed; who warns them while she indulges them, and sympathizes with them while she remonstrates with them; who

superintends the use of the liberty which she gives them, and teaches them to turn to account the failures which she has not at all risks prevented; and who, in a word, would cease to be a mother, if her eye were stern and her voice peremptory. If all this be so, it is plain that a certain tenderness, or even indulgence on the one hand, and an anxious, vigilant, importunate attention on the other, are the characteristics of that discipline which is peculiar to a University. And it is the necessity of the exercise of this elastic Rule, as in a good sense of the term it may be called, which is the great difficulty of its governors. It is easy enough to lay down the law and to justify it, to make your rule and keep it; but it is quite a science, I may say, to maintain a persevering, gentle oversight, to use a minute discretion, to adapt your treatment to the particular case, to go just as far as you safely may with each mind, and no further, and to do all this with no selfish ends, with no sacrifice of sincerity and frankness, and with no suspicion of partiality. [4]

This passage from one of the greatest of Catholic educators might well serve us as a final reminder that Catholic college discipline is bound up with the striving for Christian perfection not only in those who are bound by the rules, but in those who make them and apply them as well.

---

[4] *Ibid.*, pp. 116-17.

PART II
Summaries of Seminar Proceedings

The Seminar on Teaching English Composition Integratedly

Session I

The teacher who wishes to present his course in English composition integratedly will give his class an awareness of the role that this course in the craft of writing plays as part of the student's preparation for his fourfold vocation of priest-prophet-maker-ruler which has been described in previous workshops. The student must come to a realization of the fact that the development of his talent in the art of expression is a basic necessity for all of his college courses, which together are designed to develop in him the full man who will do his part in sacramentalizing the world and in restoring all things in Christ. In his apprenticeship as a writer, the freshman will be encouraged to become as eloquent in presenting the truth as he is able through a clear, accurate presentation so that he will be able to fulfill his vocation as priest-prophet-maker-ruler.

The teacher of English composition can assist the beginner in his mastery of the writer's craft by arousing within the neophyte's soul an enthusiastic desire to bring whatever morsel of truth he can to the hungry minds of his fellowmen. He can aid the student beset by nameless fears by pointing out to him that he is not expected to have or to acquire the literary expression of a genius like Newman, but that he will be expected to develop his natural powers of communication so that he will be able to convey to others in clear, direct, idiomatic prose the truth which he has apprehended. Through wise direction and exercise, the teacher brings the student to a realization of the growth of his native abilities in communicating truth and thus stimulates the fledgling writer to make new and greater efforts in mastering the art.

Besides dispelling any misconception of his ability to write and stimulating the student's enthusiasm for the acquisition of facility in expressing himself, the teacher must show by concrete example what unemotional, straightforward prose is. He must give the student the opportunity of exercising himself in this mode of expression under his wise guidance. Repeatedly, the teacher will urge the apprentice-writer not to indulge in mere self-expression, but prompt him instead to apply all his powers in conveying the truth that will satisfy a need existing in his fellowman. As the student sees his writing taking on purpose, he finds that expressing himself with simplicity and directness comes more naturally. It is thus in making his writing purposive that the teacher aids the freshman in integrating his course of composition into his life.

Session II

The teacher of English composition can train the student in simple, straightforward prose by exercising him in the writing of a piece that conveys information or advice. Since man is fundamentally a causal creature, an exercise in informative writing which defines a thing in terms of its purpose, rather than in terms that merely describe, aids the student in communicating an idea directly and clearly. To demand of the student an article that aims at molding a man, so that he will act in accord with some suggestion, enables him to achieve a directness basic in the art of communication. Most important of all, the student in writing informative or advisory selections exercises himself in that practical Christian charity that satisfies another's need and, at the same time, eliminates a concentration on self that blocks a proper integration of his own personality.

For the freshman in the liberal arts course, the composition course serves as an instrument of integration in a particular way in that it brings him to a realization of his role in the divine plan of the universe. The student can be shown that Divine Providence has ordained that man is a cosmic creature in whom the whole cosmos is sublimated and perfected, for in man only among creatures of the earth does the whole of creation become intelligible and capable of appreciation. And he, the spokesman of creation, can show that intelligibility and appreciation of the divine plan in his writings. Furthermore, in the divine order of things, the student sees himself as a helpmate of his fellowmen; he realizes that no action of his ever merely begins and ends in himself. His course in composition is integrated more fully as he begins to discard ideas that are individualistic and begins to see himself in what he expresses in the proper relationship of himself to God and man. He sees too that in his exercise of self in the craft of communication that he must help others so that they may better realize their vocations as well. Hence, the young craftsman learns to cast the matter of his composition into such a form as will bring his fellowmen to think and act in accord with the role that God has planned for them. Man, by nature reflective, in reading what he has written will apply the matter to himself and arrive at an application that fits himself. With such ideas of the value of his course, the student sees himself and exercises himself not in mere writing, but in a writing that integrates his whole personality a bit more fully for his vocation as priest-prophet-maker-ruler.

Turning from general considerations to practical and concrete particulars that will aid the teacher in his guidance of the student in the mastery of the craft of writing, we find that the teacher may, quite effectively, give the student an analysis of ordinary prose in terms of the fourfold causality of Scholastic philosophy. In these terms, the subject matter of the ordinary composition will be the material cause; the form into which it is cast, the formal cause; the technique used in presentation, the efficient cause; and the purpose and its application to the mind of the reader, the final cause. To grasp fully this causality found in the act of writing of ordinary prose, an analysis of ordinary prose such as has been devised by Mr. John Julian Ryan will be of great value.

GENERAL ANALYSIS OF ORDINARY PROSE

FINAL CAUSE	|	MATERIAL CAUSE
	Patron	*Subject matter*
To enable reader to get and to appreciate gist of some new discovery or situation	SELF — interested in truth and goodness	Practical and speculative science and wisdom
	Will — submissive, alert, (possibly) anxious	Directions and commands
To visualize alternatives and consequences	*Intellect*—having one cogent idea; following reason to get to the point (unity, order)	Sound inferences, universal principles, essential definitions, distinctions, classifications
To define policies or to make commentaries		
To diagnose and to recomment	*Judgment* — suspended, alert, evaluative	Sound norms, crucial instances
To give information To give advice	*Memory* — active, well-stocked	Facts, evidence
	Cogitative sense — alert, asking what's best to be done here or how does this fit into general principles (Collative sense)*	Puzzles and suggestions
	Imagination — flexible, not easily shocked; trained in given field	Implications, daring hints, hypotheses, analogies, novel facts
	Senses — hearing (mildly and negatively interested)	

* See article in *Modern Schoolman* on cogitative sense, March and May, 1944 issues.

FORMAL CAUSE	EFFICIENT CAUSE
Form	*Technique*
Reportorial or advisory writing; articles	Explaining and aiding (Do not underestimate reader's intelligence, nor overestimate his knowledge.)
Challenging, brief, stream-lined, compact, tactful, easy transitions	Limiting the discussion generally
Simplicity, proportion, neat correlation, evenness of meaning, clarity and orderliness	Analyzing, classifying, defining, distinguishing, discovering implications, hypothesizing, judgment and evaluating
Measured phrasing, calmness, dispassionateness, impersonality	Estimating reader's knowledge in each given point
Whole before parts, decision before reasons, assumptions, summaries, repetitions, transitions	Eliminating the devious and irrelevant
Proverbial utterances, technical warnings, saws	Acts of correlating, condensing, and amplifying
Neat, dry, crude, exact examples	Memorizing (Student writes without notes in class.)
Simple, inconspicuous, level music with relatively short cadences; quietness	Outlining (inductively, deductively)

	Revising
	  a. Redoing the whole
	  b. Checking it for lumps in meaning; cacaphonies

Session III

(In this session the Seminar directed its efforts towards practical methods of developing the student's ability to write. Mr. Ryan outlined a method summarized here which he has found successful in teaching creative writing.)

The apprentice in the art of writing can gain much from a study and practice of the method which the professional writer employs in writing an article for a magazine. The professor may proceed in exercising his class in this method somewhat as described in what follows. The teacher asks the student to write a letter to an editor of a magazine of his choice in which he proposes to write an article containing the points which he outlines therein for this publication. This letter is submitted to the teacher who comments or suggests on the proposed article and returns it to the student for a 1500 word draft. Working on the principle that no student in his first draft will achieve the requisite quality in his composition, the teacher returns the draft after four or five days so that the student may rewrite it with a new approach to the subject. The second version is followed by a third in the following week; this latter the teacher criticizes from the standpoint of an editor, but more so from the position of an interested coach of the one mastering new techniques. This method of writing an article, which bridges a period of four weeks, may be employed throughout the freshman course in English composition.

As may be rightly supposed, students do not readily take to the four step method of learning the craft of writing, especially not to the 1500 word assignment. The wise teacher will have to use his ingenuity to dispel the various fears and possible discouragement to which most students succumb. The apprentice in the art of communication needs pedagogical encouragement in his ability to express himself in an article of such length. He needs to be urged not to center his attention upon the actual motions he must go through in the writing process, but upon the ideas which he wishes to convey to the minds of his readers. Fear of the proportions of the task must be dispelled by showing him the suitability of the 1500 word article in dealing adequately with a topic and by making him aware of the fact that any aritcle is made up of several points, each of which is to be illustrated by two or three examples. Thus, through the teacher's stimulation to self-confidence and awareness of the simple steps that make up a major task, the student frees himself from the shackles of fear.

The problem of what topics to assign frequently troubles the instructor of the English composition course. Besides the topics of interest that the student may choose of his own accord, Mr. Ryan suggests he should be asked early in the course to write an autobiography and later a plan of his life fifteen years from the present. The advantage of the former assignment lies in that it gives the teacher a better understanding of the student; the advantage of the latter in the fact that it matures the student in that he must plan the future. In these two types, as in all assignments, the principle aim always must be that of giving the student the best possible means of developing his powers of expression.

After the question of assignments had been settled, the seminar turned its attention to the various techniques such as punctuation, jargon, syntax, classification, and transitions which are used in the writing process.

A perennial difficulty for almost every teacher of English composition is that of educating the freshman in simple rules of punctuation that he should have learned before entering college. A rather simple method that dispenses with the many rules that are found in manuals of composition is that of teaching the student that punctuation serves the purpose of indicating pauses of varying length. Thus the rules for the use of commas, semicolons, colons, and periods can all be summed up in a few rules which consider each of these marks as either one, two, three, or four stop pauses.

Session IV

A practical rule for the correct usage of the comma is that of considering it a short, one-beat pause that is indicated for the listener's convenience. It is used in the following instances:
> to indicate that the words are out of their normal order;
> to indicate that more than the requisite number of words are used for subject, predicate, or object;
> to indicate the distinct thought units of two sentences

that are easily grasped and are joined by *and, or, but* or *for;*

to indicate separate and distinct units, e.g., "There were two men, John and James," as contrasted with "There were two men, John, and James" (2 men or 4);

to set off a phrase which is longer than the mind is accustomed to grasp in normal circumstances.

Turning to the semi-colon, we see that it is a slightly longer or two-stop pause that supplies the connection for *and, or, but,* or *for* which is omitted, and that it signifies a more formal connection in a compound sentence, e.g., "He was weary; therefore he sat down." Still longer is the pause which a colon represents; it is used to relate things that are too difficult to handle with simpler marks of punctuation such as an enumeration or a formal introduction to some matter.

Somewhat akin to the confusion that exists in the mind of the college freshman at the beginning of his English composition course is the confusion that is in his mind regarding jargon. Or it is ignorance of its very existence? Its common usage indicates laziness or sentimentality on the part of the writer. If due to laziness, it is manifested in the mixed metaphor, the tired, abstract mode of expression, and the vague generalization. If due to sentimentalism, it breaks out in formal or pompous expressions, those that are prudish, falsely polite, packed with the extra thrill, or those characterized by unrestrained emotion. The student must be made aware of the fact that such emotionalism in writing is characteristic of the adolescent and not the mature mind. He must learn to rid himself of details that are expressive of personal feelings and to employ expressions that arouse the proper emotional response on the part of the reader. An excellent method of demonstrating the difference between jargon and good writing is that of showing the student the difference between the two as manifested in a good sports article and one that is written in jargon.

Session V

The teacher of English composition who merely assigns a topic to the student usually finds that the latter hands in a compilation of random thoughts on a subject that lacks value. A better method is that of having the student write on some point or statement about a topic. After the assignment has been given in this definite way, the student is to make an outline of the steps he will take in developing it. Mr. Ryan suggests that the student be taught how to concentrate his attention not on the words or the turns of phrases he is employing, but upon his outline as a problem in design which can be formulated by answering the "formula of the four abouts," which may be stated as follows:

What topic am I going to write about?
What am I going to say about this topic? — What is my main point?
What minor points am I going to make about this main point?
What am I going to say about each of the minor points?

When these questions have been answered in an orderly development, a summary of them is written to conclude the article.

Another technique that may be used by the student in making a satisfactory plan or design for his article is that of making up a series of questions on the subject which the ordinary person would like to have discussed. These questions may be answered as an expert would answer them and the answers may be arranged and developed as a feature-article writer would organize them.

A third technique incorporates the method of the "abouts" and the series of questions. The former is used to organize the answers that have been given to the questions.

The study of syntax proves valuable to a student in learning how to define and correlate things adequately. It does this in teaching him proper agreement, proper subordination, and the elimination of the dangling modifier. As regards agreement, in his study the student learns to concentrate on eliminating bad habits of equating things that are different, e.g., a noun with an adverb in the sentence, "Spring is when boys play ball." He learns to equate only words that are of the same kind so that a proper parallelism of structure is found in his sentences. As the apprentice studies proper subordination, he discovers that words of greater importance are to be given the more important position, that a series of steps in thought rise in climatic order, that there must be a proper sequence after introductory words of time, that the cause or the effect will be emphasized according to importance of either, and that accidental relationships of things are given a place of lesser importance.

Session VI

Not only does the student find that a mastery of correct punctuation is valuable in the correlation of ideas, but that is helpful in giving him a sense of the music of good prose. It teaches him something of the rise and fall that must exist in a good sentence, e.g., in the sentence, "The sun has set; the wind has fallen." Practice in the amplification of simple sentences devoid of punctuation into larger units with multiple and varied punctuation gives the student a realization that there is usually a point of emphasis before or after the mark of punctuation, and that the more pauses for punctuation, the more points of emphasis and points of rise and fall. As the student gradually achieves well-wrought sentences possessing a certain cadence and a more melodic prose, he begins to have a greater professional freedom in the placement of words; he departs from the ordinary subject-predicate-object word order; he gleans, finally, the facility with more generic terms and is forced to think.

In addition to training in outlining an article, the undergraduate must be acquainted with the art of classification so that he will be able to arrange and order his thought. As the scientist or the merchant fails without some principles ordering the particular science or business, so too the student with a motley collection of notes lacking logical headings and subdivisions is doomed to confusion and failure. Classification, though often mistakenly identified with the outline of an article, is concerned with the ordering of ideas; an outline is concerned with the diplomatic placement of points that will win a reader. The former is strictly logical; it avoids all comments. The latter emphasizes one or more points of a classification and disregards or gives only cursory treatment to the others. To achieve a correct arrangement of major and minor divisions of a

subject the following principles of classification may be used as a test in the ordering process:
1. Use one method of subdivision at a time;
2. Exhaust the possibilities of that method;
3. Make sure that the subdivisions are parallel and exclusive;
4. Make sure that the subdivisions are parallel in phraseology;
5. Make the major subdivisions before the minor (and beware of lists);
6. Make sure that the subdivisions are congruent with that which they subdivide.

Session VII

Another method of classifying is that of examining a topic in the light of the six questions that may be asked about anything, namely: when? where? who? how? why? what? These questions are listed in the first of three columns while the second and third are used to record the method and application of the same. Using the topic "College Athletics," this system may be illustrated as follows:

QUESTION	METHOD	APPLICATION
When?	Times	Those played in fall only Those not played in fall only
Where?	Places	Indoors Outdoors Indoors and outdoors
Who?	Persons	Those played by the physically robust only Those not . . .
How?	Manners or ways	Those employing rhythm (regular or spasmodic) Those not . . .
Why?	Purposes	Primarily recreational Not primarily recreational
What?	Things or means	Games employing ballistic things Games not employing . . .

Many more possible considerations could be worked into this illustration than those listed. The value of this framework for classifying lies in the fact that it obviates easy generalizations that make poor classifications.

A further method of training classification is that of taking a list of words and listing them under one generic and as many specific subheadings as possible. For example, the words "bell, flashlight, cane, and seeing-eye dog" could be classified under the generic heading of "means of guidance." As such means they may, for example, be divided into means employing sound (bell) or not, into the living (dog) and the non-living, into those primarily for the sighted (flashlight) and those that are not. The value of such an exercise in classification lies in the fact that it gives the student a great flexibility of mind that he cannot obtain any other way.

The application of classification to a group of synonyms can be further training in this art and can serve as a means of building a more precise vocabulary. Synonyms belonging to one generic group are characterized by a difference that conveys a precise meaning in which each differs from the rest. To demonstrate: "to bestow, to grant, to confer, and to present" are all synonomous with "to give." Subjected to classification, they may be listed as verbs that imply a special need on the part of the recipient (to bestow, to grant) and those which do not (to confer, to present). Those implying a need are subclassified into giving upon request (to bestow) and the opposite (to grant). Those implying no special need are subdivided into giving that implies an honor (to confer) and into giving that need not necessarily imply it (to present). The apprentice-writer profits from this exercise particularly since it gives him a realization that synonyms are not mere substitutes for the same idea. More cautious and more precise habits of employing these words are developed from such a realization.

A final method of classification is that of applying what may be gleaned from the statements of five persons in an imagined conference on the subject. The student mentally notes the comments that each member of a group would make on a given topic and uses this variation in comment as a plan for his subject. Having thus dialectically determined various viewpoints on the subject, he develops a classification according to personal opinions on the matter.

No matter which of the methods of classification are

utilized, the important matter in developing the ability of the student is that of giving him varied exercise in classification so that he develops a clarity and precision of thought for writing.

Session VIII

Important as the proper organization and classification of material are for good writing, the proper execution of a good piece demands that there be satisfactory transitions from one idea to another which serve as directives to the reader in his mental journey through an article. The value of transitional expressions is seen in the fact that the great writers rely heavily upon them for clarity of presentation; Newman, to cite a pertinent case, uses one third of his words either to advance or to summarize his work. Necessary as experssions that carry the mind forward are, they must be used skillfully and unobtrusively. So utilized, they may be of two types: the thematic which gives the order of discussion, the importance of the subject, and the reason for the order; and the panoramic which gives the reader a general view of the whole matter. Whether thematic or panoramic, transitions achieve a definitely superior quality when they are not the ordinary expressions indicating an advance but are made up of smooth flowing expressions that imply progress. Practice in inserting such thought steps into ones own compositions and the study of men like Beerbohm, Belloc, and Arnold will prove profitable to any writer intent upon mastering transitional devices that slip the mind of the reader from one idea to another without notice.

Worthy of special consideration are the various devices of transition that may be used to promote intellectual progress in an article. Some of these are repetition, associational links, the categories of logic, and the cadences of good prose.

To begin, the repetition of an idea, in identical words or, better, in equivalent phraseology, has the effect of imparting strength to an idea. Such repeated projection of an idea in different garb has the advantage of fixing the importance of the idea upon the reader's mind.

Less obvious, hence smoother in presentation, is the use of associational links or words that suggest related ideas in advancing the mind from one part to another in an article. An expression may be associated with another because it seems to suggest synonymity, similiarity, contrast, rhyme, or contiguity with the word used. Or it may move the mind onward because it brings up relationship of cause and effect, of whole and part, of concrete and abstract, or of genus and species. The possibilities open to the writer through associational links open up many interesting ways of advancing thought.

Quite practical too in indicating transitional steps in writing, though seldom presented for that purpose, are the categories of Scholastic logic. These categories are suggestive of substances or things, of various qualities associated with a subject, of variation in quantities, of different places and times, of dispositions, of relations, of accessories or instruments employed, of actions, and of passions. The worth of the categories as words possessing the power of promoting ideas becomes apparent when a list of words that can be classified under each category is made.

Finally, among the modes of transition touched upon here, there is the very subtle type that is achieved in a skillful use of cadence. By a skillful balancing of sound and the natural variations found within the sentence, the writer can get great variety in his presentation that can advance his idea marvelously. The re-arrangement of words of a sentence so as to denote a rising quality can advance an idea; that which gives the fall of normal speech can retard or bring finality to an idea.

Final Session

In the final meeting of the seminar on English composition the use of the thematic sentence in the writing of an article and the use of dynamic stress in presentation of an idea were discussed.

A thematic sentence that serves as a guide for writing can be obtained on a given topic by recording the ideas that occur to the mind on the subject on a sheet of paper and then restating these ideas in one sentence in which all but the principal idea is subordinated. This sentence is placed on a sheet of paper as the general statement of the article. On succeeding sheets are placed specific details contained in the clauses of the sentence, and on a third section of sheets particular ideas occurring under the specific details. These sheets form the guide for the actual writing process.

Dynamic stress is a principle used in writing that takes cognizance of the emphasis that is found in the beginning and end of a sentence and uses these points to exhibit the more important words or ideas. A mediocre grouping of words can be made more attractive and forceful by a rearrangement of ideas so that the important elements have a dynamic position through a placement in those positions where they will receive the stress.

The seminar ended with an analysis of terms that are frequently employed in examination questions given to determine the precise meaning of the same so that the proper method of answering the questions could be passed on to the student.

Seminar on Integrating the Social Sciences

Integration is a requisite of life itself, both on the natural and the supernatural levels. Interacting physical, biological, mental and social forces lead to destruction unless they are coordinated to weave an integrated pattern. Any education, therefore, which is meant to have bearing upon life should seek to produce well integrated minds and personalities imbued with respect for the proper hierarchy of values and for the order which makes life a thing of harmony and beauty. College education in particular offers unique opportunities to inculcate within the minds of students the principles which govern harmonious living, principles which find their roots in Christian doctrine and in philosophy, but which find their implementation through the sciences, the humanities, and all the disciplines that look into the multiple phases of reality.

Within the total plan of integrated education and life the social sciences occupy a position of enormous and ever increasing importance. Speaking in terms of horizontal and vertical integration, we find them first on the vertical plane receiving constant directives from moral and supernatural principles above them, and in turn applying these principles to innumerable and often critical issues on the level of reality below them. On the horizontal plane the social sciences are closely linked with the humanities, the physical and biological sciences, and whatever disciplines may form a part of college training. As many teachers will acknowledge, students themselves perceive the need for such two-fold integration as they advance in learning.

The integration of the social sciences with religious and moral principles and with life, as also their integration among themselves and with other disciplines, can be achieved through any number of educational techniques. This seminar brought its attention to bear upon several of these.

(1) First is was unanimously agreed that a course in Christian social principles should be made a requisite for all freshmen college students. This course, which might be called *Social Principles, Social Ethics, Social Reconstruc-*

tion, etc., should be fundamentally Christian, stressing the social doctrine of the Church, with lesser emphasis on the principles of philosophical ethics for which the young students are insufficiently prepared. It should include enough descriptive material and provide enough elementary knowledge of actual facts to carry over effectively into future social studies and social life. Such a course should be taught preferably by a member of the social science department or division, though the teacher must be well versed in the theological and philosophical doctrines related to his own field. At least four semester hours should be required for it, and six hours would not prove excessive. It is not meant to replace any part of the religion course or of philosophical ethics, but it should serve as an introductory course with a view to integration with the students' formal studies and personal reading and experience.

(2) This seminar further agreed on the need to establish or to improve the college community. The expression "college community" carries a broader meaning than "student community," embracing as it does the faculty members, the administration, and the entire life of the college. Of course, such a community is not urged merely as a proving ground or experimental laboratory for the social sciences. It constitutes an ideal incorporating the best in those Christian traditions which evoked the cry: "Behold how these Christians love one another." The social, the economic, and, in a sense, the political life of the campus must bring students and faculty together in charity, fairness, and cooperative effort. Unorganized and informal activities on or off the campus, in recreation, in group study and discussion, in visits to the poor, the sick, the prisoners, in solving one another's financial difficulties, etc., these as well as organized clubs and associations, including the Y.C.S. and student government, are well-known means of creating and stimulating the desired community spirit. But in all aspects and phases of college community life the ideals of Christian social living must ever be recalled and reapplied both by faculty and students. No better proving ground can be provided for the social sciences.

Care should be taken, however, not to tie up the students with the college in such a manner as to break their relationships with the parish life which will remain their Christian community in later years. They should be constantly encouraged by the college to collaborate in parish activities and with parish authorities.

(3) This seminar discussed at some length the advisibility of student participation in the welfare work of various Catholic and non-Catholic agencies, or in such organizations as the Catholic Labor Alliance. Though it was easy to agree that such participation constitutes valuable experience and often provides opportunities for the exercise of true apostolate, there was considerable hesitancy about the whole matter. One member of the seminar recalled the useful distinction between living and non-living laboratories: volunteer workers are not assigned to the operating room. Likewise, the well-meaning student may not always be ready for active participation in social endeavors. The college authorities must evaluate the usefulness of a project, its inherent dangers, and must maintain careful supervision over it. Activities within the students' own local community,—town or parish—should receive preference over the others because the students will probably acquire more understanding and prove more valuable as helpers in their own familiar environment.

(4) Individual counselling as proposed by one member of the seminar appeared to all as a very useful technique for integration. At the college described by the seminar member, the dean is responsible for most of the counselling, though the major professors offer guidance in their own fields to junior and senior students. The trying and time-consuming work required from the dean in such a plan is considered worthwhile and rewarding.

(5) The classroom technique of referring to the social problems faced by the students in their own environment had been found very effective by one seminar member as a means of integrating the social sciences. Such problems, by their very nature, cross the boundaries of isolated disciplines and often find their solutions in the principles of Christian social living. The study of a real and sometimes personal situation also stimulates interest and often reveals astonishing abilities of observation and analysis in the students.

(6) Some attention was given to survey courses as a means of integrating the social sciences. The seminar found

that much can be accomplished by a survey course within one department, such as history or sociology. The survey course serves as an introduction for those later to specialize in the field, while it is the most satisfactory plan for the other students who will follow no further studies in the same line. The broader survey courses embracing several specialized areas, such as sociology, economics, political science, are yet in the experimental stage at certain colleges and further information is needed about their operation and outcomes. Considered theoretically they seem to hold much promise.

A final note must be added on the value of good courses in religion, Christian doctrine, or theology, to integrate the students' lives and their studies, particularly their social studies. At one college represented in the seminar the four-year theology course serves this purpose very effectively, and the students themselves acknowledge it. Many problems of integration seem considerably lessened by the co-ordinating force of religious principles.

Seminar on Integrating Epistemology, Cosmology, Chemistry, and Physics

Since all men by nature desire to know, and to know in terms of ultimate causes,[1] it is particularly discouraging that the community of human knowledge is disintegrating almost to the state of atomization. The wise ideal of distinguishing in order to coordinate, of specializing and concentrating with a view to a fuller understanding of the whole, has been somewhat lost. The growing rift between the sapiential sciences (philosophy and theology) and the empirical sciences has grown ever more wide. The strange result of this is that science, given a new propulsion in the past by the empiricists (e.g., Locke and Bacon) and idealists (e.g., Kant) has now been erected into an ultimate, particularly by such men as Spencer, H. G. Wells, Jeans, and Eddington.

Yet there have been notable defections from such a position back to philosophy under the leadership of such scientists as Max Planck and such philosophers as Henri Bergson and Alfred North Whitehead. More and more the extreme specialization of the sciences is demanding a unifying science and is looking frequently to philosophy for direction. There is a cry for integration.

The following, the results of a ten-day seminar, consists of a consideration of the problem, some conclusions attained, some suggestions proposed. The development consists of (1) a consideration of the epistemological factors; (2) the distinction of the sciences; (3) cosmological factors; and (4) conclusions.

Epistemological Factors

In any attempt at coordinating and integrating philosophy with the physical sciences, it would seem most logical to begin with epistemology. This is the case since cosmology and the physical sciences treat of the same material object, the world immediately or mediately perceptible to the senses. Their differentiation should be that of

---
[1] Aristotle, *Metaphysics*, L. I. C. 1,980ª22.

intellectual approach as directive of the course of method. Hence, it appears logical to begin with investigating the methods peculiar to philosophy and to the physical sciences in order to see how these methods, of themselves, either ascertain certitude or approach it in a high degree of probability.

The first thing, then, under consideration is the question of the nature of certitude and probability. The former is defined as "a firm adhesion of the mind to a proposition without prudent fear of error." The latter is defined as "a more or less strong inclination of the mind towards a proposition with a prudent reservation concerning error." The kinds of certitude are metaphysical, based upon the very existence of things; physical, based upon the natures of things; and moral, based upon evidence as a motive of intellectual acceptance.

Applying the existence of such certitude to the philosophical and scientific disciplines, we can see the results by contrast. The philosophical method is that of abstractive analysis having as its end the discovery of the nature of a thing. If this analysis or abstraction is sufficiently penetrating, then there is the possibility of accurate and true deduction; that is to say, the application of a universal principle to individual cases. It is to be noted, however, that before this is possible, the analysis must attain to the nature, if possible to the specific nature and at least to the generic nature, in order that the knowledge obtained, *of itself* and without interpolation or extrapolation, make the concept universal. Thus, a mere counting of men will never allow us to say that all men are mortal. We must have sufficient knowledge of man's nature, at least to the extent that we see him capable of resolution into parts, which is mortality.

The scientific method, on the other hand, puts such emphasis upon analysis in the nature of its work that it reduces it almost to articulation. The method, briefly, is that of presumption of first principles, observation of a repeatedly attractive fact, selection of data and elimination of non-pertinent factors, hypothesis, testing, and possible confirmation of the hypothesis by experimentation or closer observation, erection into a theory as long as it can: (1) accurately reproduce all experiments concerned, and (2) predict. Any variance in these norms, as well as any discovery of new and varying facts or factors can bring about the complete abandoning of the theory or (much more likely) the absorption of it into a new theory. Since we can always expect the discovery of new facts and factors, we can always expect scientific theories to change by way of progression.

Thus we must note that: (1) since scientific theory is based upon certain presumptions, e.g., the order in the universe, causality, etc., and since (2) it always involves counting and selection of cases (and hence is not exhaustive in its considerations), *of itself* it can only grant a high degree of probability.[2] The observer, the scientist, might possess, as a result of his work and his theories, moral certitude. Yet, that is not from the theory but from what the theory supposes by way of presumptions. Thus, although we know that in a very short time some cosmic event might disturb our solar system sufficiently to destroy the earth, yet we are certain that the sun will rise tomorrow, and the certitude comes from ourselves rather than from any astronomical theory.

The calculus of probabilities that is so necessary for a scientific theory introduces the necessity of mathematics. In discussion it was seen that all forms of mathematics reduce themselves to two sources: (1) the laws of number and attempted computations, arithmetic, algebra, etc.; and (2) measurements, the various geometries. The union of the two, so characteristic of the calculus, is the work of analytic geometry in order that in the discoveries of science a more accurate and more precise tool might be devised for measurement and for the formalized concepts of measurement.

Mathematics is at once (1) the extremely precise recording and directing tool of the physical sciences, and (2) the formal object of the sciences. This factor is pointed out at great length by Maritain, but it is an old one, probably

---

[2] It must be noted that these conclusions are restricted to chemistry and physics. Other of the sciences, particularly biology and the scientific aspects of medicine, sometimes attain physical certitude. This, however, is because the investigator has attained a knowledge of the generic nature of the disease or affliction, its causes, etc. An example of this is the knowledge we have of the various hookworm diseases.

originating with Aristotle and certainly stated expressly by St. Thomas Aquinas.[3]

Today, so much of contemporary scientific philosophy is simply the formal aspect of mathematics, particularly, tensor calculus. That this is the case is largely the fault of the philosophers, particularly those latter scholastics who allowed the grand science of reality, scholastic philosophy, to descend into a system of logic. This paved the way for the empiricism of Bacon and Locke, which in turn gave way to the idealism of Berkely, the scepticism of Hume, and the *a priori* subjectivism of Kant, who, in particular, has had a tremendous influence on contemporary "philosophies of science." That process is a logical procedure. If empirical philosophy denies man the ability to discover the nature of reality and thereby *to discover* the absolute, in his quest for an ultimate answer man will *erect* an absolute, either out of ideas or out of method. So much so is this the case that we can safely classify our theoretical scientists into predominantly one of three classes:

1. The idealists, mathematical idealists, who maintain that reality consists only of ideas, and in their own case, disengaged mathematical forms. For them, the laws of nature are but laws of statistics.

2. The empiricists, who maintain that mathematics is a science of logical possibility, the actuality of which can be guaranteed only by experimental confirmation.

3. The positivists, who identify truth with scientific method. Since scientific method is necessarily mutable by progression, truth, for the positivist, is essentially progressive.

In conclusion to this section we might say that the big epistemological problem in the physical sciences today is that of uncertainty. That is not so much the uncertainty principle of Werner Heisenberg, namely, that it is impossible to measure the position and velocity of a particle simultaneously. That is a matter of fact which might be corrected in the course of time with the discovery of new and more accurate instruments. The almost unavoidable problem of uncertainty is that of the use of mathematics as the determining factor in scientific method. If all certitude is

---

[3] Aristotle, *Physics*, Book II (entirely); Aquinas, *In Physicam Aristotelis Commentaria*, L. II; *In Trinitatem Boetii Commentaria*, Q. II, A. II.

to be based upon measurement, then, uncertainty is unavoidable, since there is always the limitation that sooner or later the dividing instrument will be larger than the thing to be divided. This horizon may be pushed back further and further, but it will always remain as a limitation as long as matter is conceived to be divisible. Hence, the most such methodology can grant is that of probability, as long as matter is conceived to be the ultimate rather than a component part of reality.

Distinction of the Sciences

A part of this investigation has been to discover the resemblances, differences, limitations of the sciences concerned. This is largely a matter of historical development in order to investigate problems as they have successively faced human curiosity. The groundwork had been done by Aristotle and is presented in his *Physics* and *Metaphysics*. It has been made more explicit by St. Thomas in his commentaries on those works.

We know, of course, that philosophy is the science of all things through their ultimate causes. This is shown to be in the case in question (that of cosmology), an investigation into the four causes and the outstanding properties of material things (extension, quantity, and motion). This, of course, must be abstract. The details are filled in by the sciences. In this regard, we may say that chemistry is the science of structure while physics is the science of process. Thus, chemistry has been concentrating upon molecular structure and has erected the theory of valency, the periodic table of elements, in order to explain the characteristics of elements and their typical combination into compounds. Physics, on the other hand, has been preoccupied with the problem of the interrelations of masses and motions, problems, which, since the time of Aristotle, drew physics into the science that it is. However, beginning with the discovery of ionization and furthered by investigations by both chemists and physicists into the nature of the atom, these sciences have, for all practical purposes, become identified in theory.

One fact to be deplored in any investigation of the relationships of philosophy with the sciences is the way the sciences have been blamed for ethical disturbances. It is becoming all too customary to condemn the physical sciences because of the huge strides made in the science of war, in industrialism, in such way that new ethical problems have arisen. We should recognize that the fault is not that of the sciences when the scientists remain within their own fields, but of mankind in failing to listen to the warnings of the moralists and failing to apply the universal standards of ethics and moral theology to the regulation of these new problems. The curbing of the proper investigations of the sciences will never bring an end to moral problems, and the development of the sciences is of too much value to man ever to be abandoned.

The sciences should be encouraged for at least two reasons. There is what we might call an esthetic reason, namely, that the sciences are a contribution to the fulness of mankind, particularly insofar as they tend, to a certain extent, to fulfill his quest for truth. Insofar as they offer man more and more facets of reality, they are, to that extent, worthy of investigation. They should be developed insofar as any man's state of life allows him to do so. The second reason is a cultural one, insofar as the sciences have given many contributions to a soundness of a way of life and a development of human ingenuity that is essential to a true and vital culture. It is the proper rule of philosophy, theology, and revelation to coordinate these into a civilization.

Common Problems of Philosophy and the Sciences

Since philosophy and the physical sciences are investigations into the nature of the physical world, it is to be expected that there are many problems that are common to both. In this project, we saw fit to investigate two: causality and entropy.

Causality is a moot point within philosophies and between philosophy and the sciences. Strictly speaking, causality does not enter into the scientific method, since the scientific method is one of enumerative analysis and not of abstraction. Causality is one of the suppositions presumed by the scientist. In philosophy, we should be willing to face the fact that a failure of definition, even a failure of understanding on the part of some authors, has done harm to the proper understanding of cause.

If a cause is understood to be a positive principle responsible for the becoming of another being, an objective sufficient reason for the becoming of something else, the state of the question might be clarified. Thus, where science can never find cause by seeking for an unvarying, even invariable A - B relationship, the philosopher should distinguish between the necessity of a cause for any given phenomenon and the frequent difficulty of *identifying* a particular cause for this particular fact. Thus, we know that if a stone comes hurtling through a window, something, some force, or some person propelled it. Yet we might never identify the particular boy who threw the stone.

Thus, with these suppositions, we should explain:

1. Matter and form as "objective principles responsible for the possibility of change and the specific character of change." Matter and form should be explained as principles of being and not components of structure.

2. Efficient cause as "the objective, sufficient reason responsible through activity, for the becoming of another being."

3. Final cause as the objective sufficient reason *why* a thing becomes or an event occurs. The key to this is to be found in appetites, i.e., tendencies, of all things entering into the becoming of the being or the occuring of the event.

The second problem considered in this section is entropy. It is an excellent example of how the sciences and philosophy can and should cooperate in mutual data. In this case, the answer is perhaps more accurately stated by the sciences than by philosophy. In philosophy we have to face the possibility that God's sustaining of the universe may involve a replenishing of energy. Science gives accurate and actual data that the tendencies of the expending of energy are unidirectional, tending to a running down of the universe.

Conclusion

The conclusion of this seminar is, of course, to go on record in favor of the integration of philosophy and the sciences. However, it seems best that the integration be not by way of a "philosophy of science." Philosophy is a science as are all of the other disciplines. A philosophy of science would be a science of sciences, that is to say, a special field within epistemology.

Since the integrating discipline should be that which supposes the least, attempts the deepest, aims at the ultimate principles, and, if sound in its foundations and development, achieves the most sublime, we have the word of the Angelic Doctor that the ultimate ordering principle is the virtue of wisdom,[4] the two scientific expressions of which are philosophy [5] and theology,[6] the former drawing its fundamental principles from the undeniable presence of being and becoming, the latter from revelation. That being the case, it is the conclusion of this seminar that integration should be by way of mutual respect for and contribution to one another of the philosophical and empirical sciences. The ultimate aim of such integrated development should be the enriching of culture for the complete perfection of man as God would have man perfected.

---

[4] Aquinas, *Summa Theologica*, P. I, Q. I, A. VI.
[5] Aquinas, *In Aristotelis Metaphysicam Commentaria*, Proemium.
[6] Aquinas, *Summa Theologica*, P. I, Q. I, A. V & VI.

Seminar on Integrating Biology, Psychology, Natural Theology, and Liturgy

Integration is a synthesis achieved within the individual and by the individual of all his faculties and pursuits towards two ends: (1) his life as an individual Catholic, for his own sanctification and salvation, and (2) his life as a member of the Church, for the good of the Church and its members. Such integration must mean specifically for the biologist that his biology, his science, is not a pursuit divorced from his religion, but becomes for him a means of serving God. It must mean too that his biology becomes a method of spreading the Faith, increasing the lists of the Church.

The integration described rests first on the understanding—the intelligence. It is a question of truth, not so much a question of the will, of piety. It can be achieved only by a firm conviction that the truth of science or biology is one with the truth of philosophy and theology, by a firm conviction that the entire body of truth—scientific, philosophical, theological—forms for him the basis of his life as an individual and as a member of the Church. The first step to such a goal must then be a training not only in philosophy and theology that is complete and thorough, but also a training in science, in biology, that is the finest in our power to give. If it is true that the better a biologist an integrated individual is, the better a Catholic he is, then anything less than expert training in biology is defective and of doubtful value to integration.

It follows from what has so far been said that the mere injection into average biology courses of a few truths from philosophy or a few analogies from our faith is not integration. It follows too that the mere indicating of relationships between biology and religion is not integration. Correlation and integration are not synonymous. It appears then that the first requisite in a program of integration is the development in the individual of the attitude, the conviction, that the pursuit of biology is the pursuit of truth; that if the individual chooses to be a biologist, a scientist, it is not only recommended, not only desired, but obligatory that he become the best biologist he can possibly become. For once the choice is made, this field becomes his life; this field becomes his means of salvation; in this field must his religion, his Faith be exercised, for he achieves his service of God as a whole man in every moment of his life, not only by religious acts, not only by formal prayer. There can be no separation between his life as a biologist and his life as a Catholic. Any program aiming at less is doomed to failure. Any program, for instance, aimed solely at protecting the biologist from the dangers of modern science is a poor one. Integration of our Faith with biology and science cannot be exclusively defensive, protective. It demands first and foremost the capture of the science for Christ—and such capture can be achieved only by actively pursuing the science to the utmost of our capacity, not merely by defending Faith against the unwarranted inroads science makes upon it. Biology cannot in this scheme be an indifferent thing which we need only disinfect. Integration demands that biology be turned to the service of God; it can hardly be so turned unless it is first possessed and possessed to the fullest.

The realization of such aims through an educational program makes it imperative first of all that the teacher of biology be an individual so integrated. How such integration of teachers can best be achieved is a problem of many facets whose solution cannot be expressed in any single formula. It is of course necessary that the teacher be an expert in the field, that the teacher be also fully trained in philosophy and theology. But knowledge is one thing, integrated understanding another. Possibly one of the more useful techniques in developing the desired teacher attitude is the formation of teacher seminars—small units with surely not more than five members per unit—for the purposes of discussing fundamental truths pertinent to the program. Such seminars should be so constructed that the members of any one unit are not from closely related fields, (the grouping of closely related fields results in "shop seminars") and they should take for discussion topics of considerably more basic and general interest than the specialized content of individual courses. It should above all be kept in mind that such seminars aim for the growth and development of the teacher.

Given a teacher that fulfills the requirements set forth above, what can the teacher do towards integration in the pupil in courses in biology? The role of the teacher here seems to be threefold:

1. teach biology as thoroughly, as capably as possible;
2. lay down in this teaching fundamental principles which tie the subject to related fields, especially to philosophy and theology; and
3. direct the student towards a firm grasp of philosophy and theology not so much as specialized subjects but as bodies of truth that pervade all other disciplines.

The first point has already been considered. The second involves the question of classroom techniques, and it must be pointed out that these techniques are not integration. They are merely devices by which integration can be built by the student. It is not a course to be mastered; integration is not something put on like a suit of clothes and casually worn; no matter how excellent or exhaustive the presentation of principles, the use of these techniques may be, the persistence of integration involves constant work, constant building on the part of the individual.

For this seminar the problem posed was the integration of biology with natural theology, psychology, and liturgy. The study of living things, like the study of all of nature, offers evidence for a Creator; that biology and natural theology therefore supplement each other is clear. Biology too offers evidence to show man's double nature—as having a body and possessing rationality. Here biology impinges on psychology. Man as seen through the eyes of all three of these fields emerges as a social individual both in his activity in the world and in his activity as a Catholic and member of the Mystical Body. Such activity, of course, as performed by acts of public worship is liturgy.

If we examine these broad relations more specifically, we find that two exceedingly basic and fundamental notions necessary to integration are these: that God is transcendent to the universe and that He is immanent. These truths are abundantly evident in biology even from a study of the smallest unit of living things. The cell, with its complexity of structure and intricacy of design, demands a Creator, and with its ample demonstration of working to an end, of teleology, makes God's immanence in living things quite clear. That this order, this interdependence, is not limited to single units such as cells but extends itself to all living things is shown by ecology. A study of the population, for instance, of such a prosaic thing as a pond of water reveals not only organization within individual things but organization and dependence of all forms on each other. The immanence of God can hardly be questioned.

Biology together with psychology demonstrated quite clearly that living things are of three kinds: plants, which respond to stimuli but do not feel; animals which respond and feel; and man, who not only responds and feels but can from such sensations derive abstract ideas, who can think, who can judge. Rational psychology further shows quite clearly that this highest ability in man lies in the fact that man's rational soul possesses an intellect and free will. It is this, the soul with its intellect and will, that sharply separates man from lower animals, and it is this separation that evolutionists do not readily admit, for evolutionists build their theory on a continuity up to and including man. If, therefore, evolution is to be held, it must be held so as to allow for a bridging of the chasm between man and lower forms by God's direct creation of man's soul. It must be held so as to maintain a difference of kind, not merely of degree, between man and lower forms.

Biology then, with psychology, quite clearly shows that man's soul is rational, immortal, and endowed with the spiritual faculties of intellect and free will. By means of his intellect man is capable of knowing truth and goodness; by means of his free will he can choose morally good or morally evil acts. This of course leads directly to a tie-up with Christian ethics. On the basis of the principles derived in this manner such problems related to biology as eugenics can correctly be solved. It was for instance pointed out in this seminar that possibly the greatest danger in the eugenics movement lies in the propaganda for selective mating—an idea that is distinctly inimical to man's nature as deduced from psychology and his exercise of that nature as shown by Christian ethics. A discussion of sterilization programs as advocated by eugenicists showed how these programs could be opposed on the basis of both ethical and biological facts.

A knowledge of man's nature from the fields of biology and psychology helps one to understand more fully the necessity of a form of worship that is external as well as internal, that is official, that is communal. The fields so far mentioned demonstrate a Creator whom man as whole man must serve and worship. For the whole man to do so, external as well as internal forms of worship are necessary. Man lives his life in a society whose members depend one on another. Man's livelihood, man's success in the world is intimately tied to his fellow-man; furthermore, man serves God as a member of His Church, His society, His Mystical Body and therefore worships Him with the society, with the Mystical Body. This demands public worship, this demands a liturgy. The symbols in liturgy are a medium for expressing abstract ideas related to our faith. Analogies drawn from biology can serve a similar purpose. Almost any truth of the faith can be illustrated beautifully by analogies from facts and processes in biology, for these are but mirrors of one and the same God. For example, the rise of sap in the tree can be compared to the flow of grace in the soul; for instance, just as nature follows a cycle in the development of the body, so the liturgy of the Church follows a cycle in the development of the soul. Or, the individual cell, with its raw materials, its enzymes, its vital principle, is an integrated unit working harmoniously towards a definite end. Great numbers of such cells, dependent one on the other, make a complex but integrated living organism. So too, the integration of biology, philosophy, and theology can make of the individual an integrated unit, and great numbers of such individuals help make the Mystical Body one harmonious organism dedicated to the service of God.

Seminar on Integrating Languages and Literatures

First Session

A series of questions to be discussed was listed. The questions concerned apparent tensions to be smoothed down and made integrable either between scientific hypothesis and faith in the linguistic-literary field, or between the modern propensities of the half-secularized students and the conservative spirit of the Church. Such questions in the range of language were: the meaning and origin of language; the sense and role of Church Latin as the center of language-integration; the linguistic comparative study of epistles, gospels, and *orationes* along with the ecclesiastical year. In the field of literature these questions dealt with the comparison of canonical and apocryphal gospel stories and the expansion of the latter into popular legends and even into great vernacular literature; the interrelations between literature and morals, poetry and mysticism, poetry and myth, myth and revelation.

Second Session

The Catholic thesis of unity of mankind and consequently of the original unity of human language is challenged by the polygenetic-linguistic theory. Furthermore, language, as a virtual system belonging to human nature, seems jeopardized by the evolutionary theory of a gradual groping for speech by imitation of animal sounds and gestures. One of the participants seemed impressed particularly by the less integrable polygenetic theory whereas another participant felt handicapped even to consider it as feeling bound to a strict belief in the literal, not aetiological, meaning of the *Tower of Babel*. Finally it was agreed that the more integrable theories had to their advantage the *reductio ad unum,* a principle by coincidence dear to modern monists. Stressing this principle and eliminating as much as possible direct apologetic tendencies seemed the generally acceptable way of dealing fairly with the questioning student, supposing, of course, that the teacher has sincerely gone through this process of integration himself.

Third Session

The ideal language used by the Catholic Church throughout the world is the Ecclesiastical Latin. Even if the situation should be changed, due to the hoped for growing expansion of the Oriental liturgies to be united with Rome or to the possible admission of the Vernacular, the Occidental student has to understand that Ecclesiastical Latin still is his universal Catholic language in the present situation. On this all the participants agreed. Ecclesiastical Latin, therefore, could be made a compulsory subject for all college students. The discussion resulted in the theoretical plan that those students who had classical Latin would get an additional training in a one year course in Church Latin which—linguistically very easy for them—would mean at the same time the ideal introduction to the ecclesiastical year, the liturgical life, and the *Orare cum Ecclesia*. Students of modern languages without Latin must be given an opportunity to join optionally, but successfully, this course from their particular linguistic predispositions. To make them feel at ease in Latin, the identity with Spanish and French syntax and vocabulary must be worked out. Practically, the prayers in all of the humanities classes are to be said in Latin, and furthermore, in order to change routine into understanding, the collects for the single days, or at least for the Sundays, as belonging to the changing *proprium* ought to be added as prayer to the invocation of the Holy Spirit in class and be distributed in mimeographed form, as one participant, dean of a college, proposed.

Fourth Session

It was agreed that each language teacher in his own class of English, French, or Spanish could prepare with his pupils from time to time the gospels and epistles of ecclesiastical feasts with the aid of the new Polyglot Missal. An experiment was made with the just occurring Feast of the Sacred Heart. Wherever the English texts seemed unclear, the Vulgate, the French, the Spanish, and the Italian were consulted and the differences explained with the structure of the different languages, short of subtleties of exegesis. For instance, the English translation "that their legs might be broken and that they might be taken away" instead of "be taken down" or "removed" as compared to French *détacher,* Spanish *quitar,* Italian *rimuovere,* could be explained by the polysemy and ambiguity of a Latin verb like *tollere;* and so the advantages of a synthetical versus an analytical language were discussed. An expression like "to preach the unsearchable riches of Christ" offered an opportunity for deepening the meaning of *preach* and *unsearchable* by comparison with the French *annoncer les richesses incommensurables,* Spanish *anunciar las ininvestigables riquezas,* Italian *recare alle Genti la buona novella della imperscrutabile richezza.* It was found that the Latin *evangelizare,* simply copying the Greek *evangelizein,* could not be used transitively in any of the modern languages so that *evangelizare investigabiles divitias* either had to be circumscribed by a synonym "to preach" or "to announce," or it had to be translated by a recomposition— "to bring the good news of the inscrutable riches to the nations." As this latter was done by the Italian, it was found out that the Italian translator always checked the Greek text, whereas the other translators did not. Again it was agreed that such a polyglot preparation would at the same time deepen linguistic, liturgical, biblical, and dogmatic insights of teachers and pupils alike and prepare a good soil for the gospel when actually read on the respective feasts.

Fifth Session

The further linguistic-literary exploitation of the epistle and gospel of the Feast of the Sacred Heart led to the suspicion that some modern translations are commenting rather than literal translations. The suspicion was verified by checking on St. Thomas, "Commentary on Ephesians," 8,19. It was then worked out how the gospel words, *Et continuo exivit sanguis et aqua,* could be used for the integration of the Eucharistic legends and literary devices of the Grail story, culminating in the great Old French and German Perceval epics, up to the English Sir Galahad, to

Tennyson and Richard Wagner. During this discussion, one of the most recent modern theories that the Grail King, being lame, could not be a symbol of Christ could be rectified by a participant who had been in the Orient. She knew that the form of the Russian Cross actually is based on a tradition of the lame Christ, the culmination of *exinanitio*. At this point the question came up whether a too much integrated course concerned with secular subject matter could not be harmful or even distasteful to the majority of the non-spiritually minded students. Most, if not all of the participants, seemed to be of this opinion. It was stated that nobody knows whether Catholic education today wishes the humanities to be an object of serious secular knowledge in harmony with faith, or only a bait for spiritual training. This kind of integration, however, would lack fundamental sincerity.

Sixth Session

Nothing is better, it was argued, to make clear what is a literary artifact than the study of some of the collects with their rhythmical-syntactical arrangement of the thoughts unfolding into a dignified, well rounded prayer. Its rhetorical beauty belongs as much to the *missarum solemnia* as the gold of the chalice and the splendor of the vestments. The *Orationes* of *Fidelium Deus omnium conditor et redemptor* and *Gratiam tuam quaesumus, Domine, mentibus nostris infunde* were studied according to *cursus planus, velox* and *tardus* and exhausted to their very details. The result, however, was the contention that a scientifically and practically minded generation scarcely can be brought back to God through all these rather complicated ways of integration. It was even hinted that things allegedly Catholic could be done in an un-American way and that a pertinent question would be whether to keep close to modern American life or to retire to the catacombs. With the loss of the real knowledge of the ancient languages, a humanistic integration in the long run would not be successful. However, something should be done with the natural sciences, as it is possible for a young girl to find God through biological experiments as well as through the humanities. Only a dictate: "Back to Latin" for the

Catholic colleges would render disputable the proposed approach.

Seventh Session

As in practice there is never a coincidence between the ideal aesthetic and the ideal moral standard, it was found that those works lend themselves best to educational purposes in which the tension between beauty and ethics is slightest. Some participants would propose to read mainly Catholic hagiographic literature. It was, however, agreed that this would not be integration but an undue extension of religious instruction, as the purpose of literary education is primarily aesthetic. No doubt that the ideal work would be Dante's *Divine Comedy*. For this, however, college girls do not seem prepared in general. The Greek and Roman Classics remain pertinent reading as they show life in its pre-Christian, this-wordly limitation, with the accent on life as not the highest value, however, if confronted with heroic transcendence of self. The idealism of English and German literature can be incorporated as far as it goes; French literature is intrinsically most Catholic, but here certain erotic implications reduce the choice to the classicism of the seventeenth century and to the contemporary Catholic revival. The proposed education with Corneille and Racine was opposed, however, as dull. In modern Spanish literature the liberal and anticlerical elements prevail to such an extent that even in that alleged very Catholic literature one has to go back to the sixteenth and seventeenth centuries. Educating with objectionable literature to be corrected by the teacher was opposed as confusing literature with sociology and psychology and ignoring the necessary sympathetic tension between subject and object of literature.

Eighth Session

It was argued that there should be used Bremond's thesis of poetry for literary education. Abbé Bremond considers poetry as a natural, synthetic intuition and vision of reality which can pertinently be explained as an analogy to the mystical, supernatural vision and intuition of the Highest Reality, God. It could be supplemented by Maritain's thesis of poetry being the translation into an artifact of a subjective truth which is not formulable in concepts. It was objected that the presentation of poetry as a higher value than material things, like food and clothing, would foster pride and produce esthetes and that detachment from higher values, if they are not religious and spiritual, would be as much mandatory as detachment from the lower ones. Today even college girls would discover the shakiness of the supposed grandeur of the Classics. It was reargued, however, that this kind of a rather pietistic criticism would make any gradation and integration of secular values and subject matter a farce. There remained the impression that the education to literary values would not work in American colleges because in literary criticism there is spoken a language too different from the language of the girls. It was reargued again that if education does not mean reshaping an erroneous reluctant mind, it does not go very far.

Ninth Session

It was discussed whether the interrelation between poetry, myth, and revelation should be fundamentally clear to a Catholic student. If so, the question arises whether in the Christian world the poet has the function of a myth-maker as he had in the pagan world where the Platonic poet transcends the philosopher by answering questions about the state of the souls after death and the cosmogony. Does not revelation take care of this? Following Professor Singleton it was possible to answer that there is room left for the Christian poet to insert his interpretative myth into revelation as can be proved, for instance, by Dante's creation of the Mount Purgatory out of Arabic and Greek elements. Making purgatory a mount he involved the truth that every ascetic purgation is a mounting and climbing higher. A mountain to be climbed is also the symbol of purgation for San Juan de la Cruz. Consequently, Dante did in the world of pertinent, i.e. mythic symbols, what the ancient poets did with the golden age symbol when they expanded on the awareness of a fallen, once happy mankind. The Christian revelation of original sin makes the pagan myth understood better than it was apprehended by the ancients themselves. The Christian poet *qua* poet cannot do anything but symbolize the truth known to him in a fuller sense by revelation.

Result of the Sessions

Ways of integration in the humanities could be shown by some fundamental, concrete examples which might be expanded by clever teachers. Thus integration in language and literature proved by all means to be a possibility.

PART III
APPENDICES

APPENDIX A

The Archives of a Catholic College or University

By Henry J. Browne

Much discussion has been devoted under the auspices of these workshops in recent years to the administration of Catholic colleges. Of necessity the keeping of records and the development of new techniques in that field have received attention. It is strange in one sense that non-current records have not been a subject of consideration; yet, from another point of view, it is very understandable. It is peculiar because old records are always with us even in an educational institution with only a few years of age to its credit. But why talk about them? Bundle them up and store them in some side room or basement or buy more filing equipment and ask for more office space. If the files are bulging, get one of the office staff to go through and weed them of material that such an individual may decide is of no lasting value, and let it be destroyed or at least stored in some inaccessible nook or corner. This spot has often been a vault, especially where old business records, the deeds to the property, or a precious looking citation received by the president of the institution was involved. But less imposing looking items—old class lists, interoffice communications, or routine letters asking for information, particularly after a change of president or dean or some other official simply become dust-laden bundles in out-of-the-way store rooms.

If this has been too often the story of the treatment of old records in our institutions, even in those of higher learning, it is, however, very easily understood in the light of the general American lack of concern for the problem until recent years. Although the historians, whose very stock in trade depends on documents, had formed a commission on public archives within the American Historical Association by 1899 and an annual conference of archivists by 1909—which was to become the autonomous Society of American Archivists only in 1937—their chief emphasis was on state and federal government archival depositories. The symbol of success for the archives movement was the opening in this country of a national archives in the nation's capital in 1935, which is now called by a title more descriptive of its full function, the National Archives and Records Service.

American colleges and universities have joined the ranks of governmental agencies, business and religious groups in the realization that something should be done to utilize the new techniques of an ancient archival profession. It was several generations ago that the materials pertaining to the history of Harvard University were gathered up by Jared Sparks to prevent their loss. Since then ecclesiastical institutions, too, have often owed the better preservation and care of their non-current official papers to the historical researchers. The Catholic University of America may be cited as an example in this regard since there is a real connection between the setting up of its Department of Archives and Manuscripts in 1949 and the fact that since 1946 four closely documented monographs on the history of its first twenty years have appeared in print. Librarians, too, have contributed to the movement and in some colleges and universities the official records of the institutions are still housed and serviced in a division of the institution's library. It has only been in recent years that the archivist as a professional servant of an institution of higher learning has come into his own. This independence of the archives agency was achieved as early as 1921 at Smith College, at Amherst in 1934, the University of Pennsylvania in 1945, Fisk in 1948, and at the Catholic University of America in 1949.

If this present paper can give some attention to and appreciation of the terms and techniques of archival economy in the United States today and can point up the need for Catholic college and university administrators to be aware of the advances made, it will have served its purpose. As a preliminary, the very notion of an archives needs a revision in many minds. It has no relation to terms like "archaeology" or "archaic," but still it conveys popularly a notion of *old* manuscripts or documents. Royal charters carrying large wax seals or ancient and indecipherable land grants are conjured up by the very sound of the word. A secret and little-frequented depository for very old and valuable written records is all too frequently the basic elements of an archives in the minds of modern administrators. This is so much a fact that business-minded people in selling what is basically the archives idea to business men have emphasized expressions like "records management."

The true definition is quite different from any "sound-meaning" and closer to the etymological one. It comes from the Greek *archeion,* meaning a government house and, hence, the papers kept therein. So it was applied at first only to bodies of official governmental documents. By analogy it was used to designate the accumulated files of an institution or even of a family. In its present American sense the plural was carried over from the French *les archives,* to mean not only the body of such records but also the place where such documents were kept. Hence, the essential element in archival material is that it be official records of a non-current nature, that is, documents produced in the carrying on of the work of a given office or agency which are no longer required for the conduct of the day to day work of that office or agency but still are of enduring value. One can realize, therefore, that the minutes of the board of trustees, the official correspondence of officers of a college or university, the individual student folders—all such—become in time archival material, although the interval will usually differ in length. They need not constitute very important material nor very old material. The word document, furthermore, does not mean only manuscripts or typescripts. There are obviously such things as an official faculty picture, blue prints, or maps not in frequent use, a bound jubilee volume, one copy of which should be preserved as a record copy, or any printed material which is issued by various offices (e.g., the catalogue of the registrar) and which ought to be preserved in one or two archival copies.

The systematic preservation and servicing of such types of official records as have been mentioned above are the real work of a college or university archives. It is true that certain other procedures have gone by the name—and all praise to those who carried them out for what has thus been accomplished in saving at least the fragmentary sources for the history of our institutions as well as of prominent Catholic figures. The vault in the library that has received the annual commencement programs or souvenirs of public receptions and, if the librarian was a "string-saver" by inclination, the menus and seating lists at various functions, this at times has been called an archives. Again the collecting propensities of some faculty member or the generosity of a benefactor may have resulted in the acquisition to the college or university library of literary manuscripts of some poet or novelist or, perhaps, the correspondence and writings of an important historical personage. These alone may have been referred to as archives or, if housed with old cold-storaged records of the institution so blessed, even said to have been deposited in its archives. In the light of the modern American professional usage which restricts archives to mean the official non-current records of an agency, such variant usages are definitely inaccurate. Administrators are no more justified in using the term "archives" so loosely than they would be in ignoring the fact that American educators now have meanings in common when they use such terms as college, or school, or faculty in connection with higher education.

But where will the manuscript gift of a benefactor be housed, and how will the historical menus be saved for posterity? The former belongs to the manuscripts division of a college or university library as much as does an illuminated medieval manuscript. The menus, like printed class day proceedings and similar material originate in some particular office of the institution and, hence, become a part of its records, and when they become unnecessary for the working of that office, if still considered of enduring value, they should be transferred as part of those records to the archives. This is just as true of the theater programs of the dramatic productions and the concert notes of the music department. These individual items are parts of larger bodies of records and the archivist, as the records officer of an institution, is not supposed to be a paper collector in the sense of being concerned with the impossible task of gathering such illusive publications as they are turned out.

The archives, then, is not intended to serve first and foremost the social scientist or critic who is interested in the examination of historical or literary manuscript materials. In this the library should and traditionally has served through its manuscript division or room. In fact, in its concern with official records the archives is fundamentally and primarily a tool of administration, and has been aptly described as the official memory of an institution. For example, Colgate and Indiana Universities have emphasized this point by the somewhat unusual step of making the archives a division of the president's office. Set up in any case as a service unit within a college or university, the archives can be made to serve as the source for the accumulated experience of that educational community. No one who has ever destroyed a letter or at times employed the telephone instead of writing is so foolish as to think that documents tell all or that men in official positions always leave behind them complete and unbiased records. It is something like the case of using examinations as the test of student ability. Everyone knows they have deficiencies but one asks immediately what else do we have. In the case of archives, what will take the place of such records? Surely not the fallible human memory!

Some services rendered by an archives are so obvious and at the same time so varied that it is not always simple to illustrate them. In an archives there is found not only a safe place for an institution's non-current legal documents but as well a place where they will be readily accessible when the school's interest calls for them. It is difficult to conceive of an administrator who at some time or other would not desire to examine at least certain records created by his predecessors to help guide his own policies. Of course, experience learned in subordinate positions in an institution may later be sufficient for wise administration at a higher level. One may hazard a guess in this regard that if complete outsiders were more commonly put in positions of leadership in Catholic colleges and universities the problem of the efficient handling of non-current but permanently valuable records might have been faced and openly discussed long before this. Apart from personal advisers, how else could traditions and precedents become known to one who was a complete stranger to the administrative family of an institution?

If ignorance of history often leads people not only into

error but even into a repetition of old errors, *a fortiori* without the sources of history—the records of an agency—an administrator may well become inflicted with a kind of myopia. Oftentimes much wisdom is based on memory. How else would one know accurately the experience of a college or university with a given individual or organization? How, for example, can an intelligent answer be given even to a problem like the reemphasizing of college football, not to mention more basic educational ones such as a reemphasis of prescribed as aganst elective courses, without a look at the past record. The question of how to celebrate the fiftieth aniversary of a Catholic college might find its answer in part by a look at the record of its silver jubilee. Naturally, such consultation will not give the complete answer, for some things like the dullness of a particular jubilee orator might be recorded only in the archives of a brain crevice of the patriarch of the faculty.

Less fanciful services, too, can be performed by a functioning archives. Such would be found in the caring for old maps and blue prints which are not constantly consulted but which are indispensable when campus alterations or expansion programs get under way. In the National Archives the availability of records of various projects such as merchant marine shipbuilding dating from World War I saved valuable time and money after the outbreak of war in 1941. In a similar way the rejected plans drawn up by an educational institution years ago may prove valuable later; or even the printed diagrams of the wiring of a building when an archivist can readily produce them may mean a great saving of expense and, perhaps, also of patience and time.

The economic argument in favor of the full-fledged archivist may best be brought home in the office of the registrar. Since it is there that records accumulate most noticeably, valuable office space as well as the work of the staff is restored for other purposes by the retirement of out-dated files. These, however, do not become dead storage but remain within easy reach for consultation and copying. The transferred student records which are within a date bracket that will see them called for only infrequently during the academic year are preserved more cheaply than in expensive filing equipment and are still readily available in an archives that is set up as a going concern. If their bulk requires, they may even be with much wisdom reduced to microfilm. This systematic release of the records pressure on this particular office is a great blessing for the registrar and an aid to the institution in fulfilling its obligation to inquiring alumni.

The purposes of a Catholic educational institution are served by an archives in less obvious ways. We may not have professors like Henry Adams whose classlists are often consulted by inquirers at the Harvard archives, but some do win sufficient fame that in later years sends researchers looking for students with some recollections of these professors. The college or university tradition on such matters as the admission of colored students will only be known faithfully from well kept archives material, although in this case, perhaps, records that are good in a moral sense will not carry the evidence. In the whole area of public relations as a matter of fact the archives can be made to serve. It may, indeed, prove indispensable for even so slight a matter as a popular anniversary bulletin, and it can be invaluable for material that is useful for exhibits or to regale old grads in alumni publications. Aims such as these have made some university archives broaden their holdings to embrace material of a less official nature relating to the history of the university; particularly appealing along these lines is a photographic archives of views of buildings and grounds and of old personnel of the institution.

There is a further and broader function for Catholic educational archives. Our Catholic educators in the past, at least by the evidence of many recent contributions to American Catholic historiography, were notoriously active in questions going far beyond the confines of their own campuses. Not only the history of Catholic education in the United States but conflicts and movements of all kinds within the Church can only be studied by research in the archives of many of our Catholic colleges and universities. Light will be found here on historical subjects as varied as the personality of Archbishop John Hughes of New York as a young priest in the 1830's to the Church and municipal politics in San Francisco in the early twentieth century. But this brings us to a service rendered voluntarily by many of our institutional archives in the interest of truth both to the members of their own schools and to serious students from outside. It is crossing over into what is really a secondary function, as even historians today are quite ready to admit.

What can be done about achieving or improving these valuable services in a college or university archives? If one were to follow the example of the University of California at Berkeley, there would be a preliminary survey made over a period of two years of the records of the entire institution. Even prior to that step of analysis there must be, of course, the appointment of an archivist. It is understandable that in a smaller institution such a person might not be able to be carried on the staff solely for that purpose. Hence, he may be connected with an administrative office, the history department, or the library, as long as he appreciates that the function he is called upon to perform as archivist is a professionally distinct one from his work in other capacities. At the very outset the archivist or records officer of any institution greatly needs a clearly defined status. He must be authorized and supported by the administration through action of the board of trustees, or at least by a directive from the office or rector or president. The archivist's position is further strengthened in some places through an archives committee made up of the principal university representatives whose interests are involved or whose advice is needed, for example, the registrar, a member of the department of history, and the librarian. These members are in addition to the archivist who should, in the ideal order, have had training, some experience, or at least the benefit of observation—if not all three—in archives administration against a background of American history and particularly, in our case, in its Catholic and local aspects.

The issuance of a charter of regulations to the record-producing offices of the institution has proved helpful in notifying the whole educational community of what the archival program aims to accomplish. In this or a similar communication, the archivist's position and full authority has to be made clear. People are at times loath to give up "old" records of a school or a department to an "outsider," no matter how ingratiating he may personaly be. Often this is based on a misconception that there is no distinction between the private papers which are a product of the personal activities of an official and the records which result from his work for the institution. These latter he has no right to destroy wilfully or to keep since they are institutional records and not his personal property. Hence the need may not be merely for an educational program but for one with some administrative teeth. The velvet glove is highly recommended as an approach in arranging for the collection of records but at times the strong hand of authority beneath it may have to be employed to get some reluctant official or professor to part with papers that he never uses, yet which he jealously guards against removal.

But despite all the glory of administrative strength, the archivist is useless without a place to work. His survey of existing records of permanent value and their rate of growth may be highly useful if plans are being drawn for completely new quarters for the new institutional service. Most of the time the necessity of adapting a vault or room will obviate concern about the exact bulk of materials to be transferred, except for the purpose of estimating the need of shelving. The important thing in such a renovation is to make the quarters safe against prying men and harmful elements such as dampness, fire, and termites. The failing of those who would maliciously destroy or remove documents as well as the type of person who would have taken the story of Judas or Peter out of the Gospels are worthy of precautions. The location of the archives should also be considered from the point of view of accessibility to the offices that will be consulting its non-current material most frequently. Another consideration is the fact that much of the searching in any archives has to be filled out with information gathered from reference books such as biographical dictionaries, almanacs, and directories. A Catholic archives would find volumes of the *Catholic Directory* almost indispensable but the library, if nearby and perhaps even preferably in the same building, would take care of that problem.

The subject of the care and arrangement of the archival material of a college or university might constitute a paper in itself. As yet there is no American handbook for the guidance of workers in this field. A few remarks of an introductory nature may, however, serve to give some guidance and at least point out possible pitfalls in the process of forming a working archives.

The survey of the archivist should in effect add to the bulk of materials which the institution's office have already decided on their own is archival. These paper-wrapped bundles contained in vaults, the old metal file cases transferred *in toto* to some closet, or the jammed transfer file cases indiscriminately piled in some other type of storage area—all such items will form the nucleus of the archives. The preliminary survey should first include such material and by consultation with the various officials in charge of them a decision may be arrived at as to whether to dispose of, select from, or transfer them in their entirety to the archives room. Furthermore, the archivist will personally have to consult with administrators about the non-current records which still encumber their offices although they are only very seldom used. These contacts should be instructive in purpose but also cooperative in spirit since his ignorance of the work of a given office may be as abysmal as the ignorance he will find there concerning archives. In the matter of inoperative items still held in office files, he might well come to a decision with the individual officials based mostly on the administrator's awareness of how often a given group of records, for example, the correspondence of his predecessors, is used and his estimation of their possible future usefulness to his own or some other office of the institution. The decision as to whether a given group of records has any permanent value over and above these considerations as, for example, for an educational or historical study, is where the records officer's experience, knowledge of the history of his institution, and historical training will be heavily drawn upon. At any rate, the records that are eventually preserved should be kept as they were originally filed. Every basic unit or records series should be integrally preserved. For example, it might be the minute books of a particular faculty or the file of correspondence of a dean's office. These should be preserved intact and no attempt should be made to integrate them with a file of someone else's correspondence, annual announcements, or any other item in a chronological or subject arrangement. The original order which an organic body of records assumed as it was being formed is sacrosanct to archivists. Any attempt to group letters by subject matter or to run together disparate materials such as alumni bulletins, promotional material, and correspondence into one file because they were produced in the same year, or to unify the records of different offices results only in archival bedlam. This statement is made with a faith that conforms to American archival practice which, in turn, has drawn on the best of a long European tradition and adapted it to the records-magnitude of our national way of life.

In this matter of accessioning material into such safekeeping, certain irregular practices follow from misconceptions alluded to above concerning the nature of an archives. A person who thinks it a place where only certain items with an immediately obvious historical or apologetic importance are filed for future use is apt to be sending to the archivist promptly on issuance all such important annoucements. Again a similarly limited idea in the mind of an administrator may result in certain choice, if not more aptly, albeit colloquially, referred to as "hot," items on some episode in the institution's past being handed over to the records agency. Such individual documents or small batches of records should rather be considered as part of a definite series of records with its own organic unity which is spoiled by such a process of selection and, perhaps, by their isolation the precious items removed are even rendered less understandable.

This preservation of records according to the office of their origin and, whenever possible, according to the order or system in which they were formed gives to the college or university archives a certain diagrammatic unity. The whole will be made up of parts which may be called record groups, the records of the board of trustees, of the president, of the various schools and subordinate departments according to date of establishment, and so on down the line of jurisdiction. Even down to the archives of the archivist the very arrangement of the records according to the best archival practice will reflect the organizational history of the college or university. Just as offices continue despite changes in personnel, so the documentary tools of their work, which are in time the chief evidence of their accomplishment, should continue in unbroken and distinct lines.

These lines of records—the so-called record groups—are not commonly retained in expensive office filing equipment in American archives. Here again the economic argument comes to the fore. Over and above the saving produced by the elimination of much useless paper from old files, under any archives program a great saving is effected even in the handling of what are considered permanently valuable records. American experience has just about established that in most cases the best containers are cardboard cartons or document cases of about five inches in width and ten in height and made to hold legal or correspondence size papers as desired. In such easily handled units the materials are shelved systematically and, if the use demands it, in time finding aids can be elaborated in the form of indices. Many times, of course, such already exist within the records transferred and remain still usable. Moreover, individual documents may be scientifically treated if they are in need of repair in order to be safeguarded against further deterioration. The old Vatican library process of silking manuscripts to preserve them against the ravages of time in the form of moisture or chemical reactions due to the ink or contact with another substance has generally given way to what is called lamination, a distinctly American contribution to archival science. In the lamination process a document is pressed between sheets of cellulose acetate foil while heat and pressure are applied until the substances become in effect blended into one. This device is merely mentioned here, not because the ordinary college or even university archives would be expected to plan for a small laminating machine, but in some cases of fragile or often exhibited documents that are highly prized by an institution, it might be well to have the manuscripts strengthened in this manner in an outside agency. Ordinarily a careful unfolding—since today's creases are tomorrow's breaks especially in modern paper—a dusting and, perhaps, first of all a fumigating, before boxing and shelving is sufficient physical processing of our ordinary types of institutional records. Within each box, of course, the division into folders as in the original filing system in the office of origin is maintained.

From what has been said it is not difficult to see that there is a very real connection between the filing of current records and the administration of an institutional archives. It can happen that some departments of a college or university may not be represented at all in the archivist's domain simply because they produced no records or at least kept none in their early days particularly. The contribution of some scientists and engineers who worked on low budgets and without secretarial staffs, one might suspect, will be lost since they are prominent in this group. Again an office with the reprehensible habit of destroying periodically enough of its old correspondence to make the file drawer a little less stuffed will certainly produce no archival material. Another bad office filing practice which militates against good current records and archives administration is simply to continue filing material without any regard to the retirement of certain amounts of material as quasi-current and eventually non-current after a determined number of years. In such cases the cabinets multiply beyond all control and when something just has to be done the situation can be handled only by a time-absorbing job of weeding. As records officer of the institution, the archivist should work out with the various agencies on the campus a program for the retirement of certain types of records to the archives and the disposal of others without transfer after stated periods of time. This is necessarily a cooperative work. Only a registrar, for instance, would know how old a student record generally is before it becomes subject to merely an occasional call. It is evident that the full meaning of modern archives administration implies this awareness of the need for the management of records from the point of origin through day to day use and on to the fires of destruction or the Elysian fields of the archives, whence, however, they may be called back at any time to serve their former masters.

It should be clear that the ultimate purpose of all archival activity is utility or service to the college or university itself. The aim is not merely to have a fine array of records but through them to supply a need which American administrators in all kinds of endeavors are becoming increasingly aware of as necessary for good administration. The secondary function of service to historical truth through aid to research is by its very statement of genuine importance. It is certainly at least not to be overlooked.

The contributions of such noted educators as Father John A. Zahm of the University of Notre Dame or Monsignor John A. Ryan of the Catholic University of America will be better known than those of some of their predecessors because their records have been preserved. The joint experiences of Catholic educators in the National Catholic Educational Association can be studied and reflected upon with profit in our day only because Catholic institutions, and these include some three educational ones, had done something to preserve their records. These are but samples of what needs little proof but they may strengthen by illustration the argument for better records and archival administration in our Catholic colleges and universities.

Archival administration is not, however, by any means a Catholic problem. Enough institutions of higher learning have already shown sufficient interest as to cause a special committee on college and university archives to be set up by the Society of American Archivists. As a matter of fact, Catholic participants in this growing professional group have not been too noticeable except for the fact that the intensive summer training program conducted by the American University at the National Archives has seen for six years now about one fifth of the enrollment representing Catholic institutions of various types. Why then speak specifically of Catholic institutional archives? It is justified if only because of the strong traditions in favor of good archival practice which are part of our sometimes forgotten inheritance. The Code of Canon Law which is the distillation of centuries of tradition legislates quite definitely on the matter for dioceses and parishes, but, of course, our colleges and institutions escape that obligation and have for the most part only the practical and even economic consideration of more effective administration to sway them to renewed interest or reform.

Yet the mid-year of the twentieth century might be a good time to advert to "impractical" considerations. "No documents, no history," is one principle we have already alluded to. If we think we have made and are making a contribution to American education, some record more than the repeated statement of the fact will be useful to the future historian. Sometimes the inquiry about the untold Catholic chapters in our American history books might be answered by the question: who has studied them or where are the sources from which one will be able to study them? When the cultural history of a nation is written, sources almost without parallel to the minds of some are found in its college and university archives. At least no one can deny that such works as Samuel E. Morison's classic volumes on the development of Harvard University or the recent history of the State University of Wisconsin or the already four-volume series on the Catholic University of America have not saved unique educational traditions from oblivion. This was made possible by the availability of the records of those institutions, but in how many of our Catholic colleges and universities will this be able to be done in such a scientific way in the next generation? Moreover, let us not lament any national shallowness which we might attribute to a lack of a sense of tradition if we do not know something of the early days and the giants of our own institutions. The pioneers and shapers of our traditions will remain unknown as will our own days, which are to be the early days to our successors of tomorrow, if our records are destroyed or simply kept stored in inaccessible places. Our roots in the past, on a very local scale to be sure, must run deep into the rich soil of our institutional archives. "What is past is prologue," wrote Shakespeare in the *Tempest,* and the government of the United States engraved it on its archives building. If some have not hesitated to cite as a measure of a nation's level of civilization its care for the written and other monuments of its past, may it not with some justice be proposed as a measure of the maturity of a Catholic college or university?

Whether from the awareness of these truths or from the very unphilosophical suggestion of a great American Catholic layman who used to call regularly for "a look at the record," it should become increasingly evident to the administrators of American Catholic colleges and universities that a well-ordered and functioning archives is not a luxury but an obligation they owe to the past, the present, and the future.

BIBLIOGRAPHY

(These items constitute a few of the sources for the above paper and also possible further readings on the subject.)

On the history of archives movement in the United States:
The National Archives of the United States. Bulletins of National Archives, Number 1. Washington, D. C.: Government Printing Office, 1936. Pp. 13.

On public and institutional records:
Brooks, Philip. *Public Records Management.* Chicago: Public Administration Service, 1949. Pp. 19.

On college and university archives:
Browne, Henry J. "A Plan of Organization for a University Archives," *The American Archivist,* XII (October, 1949), 355-358.

—————. "A Look at the Record," *The Catholic University of America Buletin,* XVIII (March, 1950), 6-8.

Jennings, John Melville. "Archival Activity in American Universities and Colleges," *The American Archivist,* XII (April, 1949), 155-163.

Mood, Fulmer and Carstensen, Vernon. "University Records and Their Relation to General University Administration," *College and Research Libraries,* XI (October, 1950), 337-345.

On archives and American Catholic history:
Ellis, John Tracy. "Can We Have a History of the Church in the United States?", *The Catholic University Bulletin,* XII (March, 1945).

O'Connor, Thomas F. "Catholic Archives of the United States," *Catholic Historical Review,* XXXI (January, 1946), 414-430.

On the administrative functions closely related to archives:
Deferrari, Roy J., ed. *College Organization and Administration.* Washington, D. C.: The Catholic University of America Press, 1947. See Catherine R. Rich, "The College Registrar," pp. 80-84; Philip Temple, "The College Library," pp. 263-286; James A. Magner, "Budget and Business Management in a Catholic College," pp. 320-333.

APPENDIX B

Members of the Workshop on Discipline and Integration in Catholic Colleges

NAME	REPRESENTATIVE OF
Sr. Mary Claire Allaire	Anna Maria College, Marlborough, Mass.
Sr. M. Aurelia Altenhofen	Rosary College, River Forest, Ill.
Sr. Margaret Mary Barrett	St. Joseph College, Emmitsburg, Md.
Sr. Mary Agnes Barry	St. Mary's College, Notre Dame, Ind.
Sr. M. Francis Bierne	Caldwell College, Caldwell, N. J.
Sr. M. Berenice Brau	Alverno College, Milwaukee, Wis.
Sr. Mary Elvira Bredel	College of St. Francis, Joliet, Ill.
Rev. Kenneth G. Bretl	Salvatorian Seminary, St. Nazianz, Wis.
Sr. Dorothy Clare Cannon	Convent of St. Elizabeth, Convent, N. J.
Sr. Mary Benedicta Carney	Mt. St. Agnes College, Baltimore, Md.
Sr. Mary Dominicus Chidester	Clarke College, Dubuque, Ia.
Sr. Margaret of the Sacred Heart Dooling	D'Youville College, Buffalo, N. Y.
Sr. M. Georgia Dunn	Rosary Hill College, Buffalo, N. Y.
Sr. Denise Eby	St. Joseph's General House, Emmitsburg, Md.
Sr. M. Regina Eckles	Mt. St. Agnes College, Baltimore, Md.
Sr. M. Maura Eichner	College of Notre Dame of Maryland, Baltimore, Md.
Sr. Bridget Marie Engelmeyer	College of Notre Dame of Maryland, Baltimore, Md.
Rev. Maurice C. Fillion	Oblante Seminary, Bar Harbor, Me.

Sr. M. Berchmans Finzel	Mt. St. Agnes College, Baltimore, Md.
Sr. Margaret Flinton	St. Joseph College, Emmitsburg, Md.
Sr. Mary Annette Gallegher	Marycrest College, Davenport, Ia.
Sr. Mary Adorita Hart	Clarke College, Dubuque, Ia.
Rev. Alfred F. Horrigan	Bellarmine College, Louisville, Ky.
Sr. M. Mildred Kalcalage	College of St. Francis, Joliet, Ill.
Sr. M. Eugenia Kealy	Marywood College, Scranton, Pa.
Sr. Rose Beatrice Keating	College of St. Elizabeth, Convent Station, N. J.
Sr. M. Eugenia Keavney	College of St. Rose, Albany, N. Y.
Sr. M. Imelda Keenan	Sacred Heart Academy, Stamford, Conn.
Sr. Mary Ellen Kelley	St. Joseph College, Emmitsburg, Md.
Sr. Margaret Francis Kelly	College of St. Rose, Albany, N. Y.
Mother Louise Keyes	Newton College of the Sacred Heart, Newton, Mass.
Sr. M. Assumpta Klimas	Madonna College, Plymouth, Mich.
Sr. Juliana Kowal	St. Joseph College, Emmitsburg, Md.
Sr. Mary Jean Leacy	Mt. St. Agnes College, Baltimore, Md.
Sr. M. Frederick Lochemes	Cardonal Stritch College, Milwaukee, Wis.
Sr. M. Inez McHugh	Notre Dame College, South Euclid, O.
Sr. Madeleine Sophie McKay	Mt. Mercy College, Pittsburgh, Pa.
Dr. George J. McMorrow	Nazareth College, Nazareth, Mich.
Sr. Catherine of Siena Mahoney	D'Youville College, Buffalo, N. Y.
Sr. M. Paul Mason	College of Mary Immaculate, W. Hartford, Conn.
Sr. M. Georgiana Mielcarek	Madonna College, Plymouth, Mich.

Sr. Teresa Aloyse Mount	Immaculata Junior College, Washington, D. C.
Sr. Margaret Gertrude Murphy	Nazareth College and Academy, Nazareth, Ky.
Sr. Josephine Pate	Mt. St. Joseph, Maple Mount, Ky.
Rev. Vincent F. Schuster	Brunnerdale Seminary, Canton, O.
Rev. Leo C. Sterck	St. Ambrose College, Davenport, Ia.
Sr. M. Joanna Tracy	Caldwell College, Caldwell, N. J.
Rev. Clyde R. Wagner	Mother of the Saviour Seminary, Blackwood, N. J.
Sr. Joan Marie Waters	St. Joseph College, Emmitsburg, Md.